Flash® Animation for Teens

Eric D. Grebler

THOMSON

COURSE TECHNOLOGY

Professional ■ Technical ■ Reference

Educational facilities, companies, and organizations interested in multiple copies or licensing of this book should contact the Publisher for quantity discount information. Training manuals, CD-ROMs, and portions of this book are also available individually or can be tailored for specific needs.

ISBN-10: 1-59863-230-2

ISBN-13: 978-1-59863-230-2

Library of Congress Catalog Card Number: 2006923273

Printed in the United States of America

07 08 09 10 11 BU 10 9 8 7 6 5 4 3 2 1

Publisher and General Manager, Thomson Course Technology PTR:
Stacy L. Hiquet

Associate Director of Marketing:
Sarah O'Donnell

Manager of Editorial Services:
Heather Talbot

Marketing Manager:
Heather Hurley

Acquisitions Editor:
Megan Belanger

Marketing Coordinator:
Meg Dunkerly

Project Editor:
Kate Shoup Welsh

Technical Reviewer:
Mark Abdelnour

Teen Reviewer:
Parker Hiquet

PTR Editorial Services Coordinator:
Elizabeth Furbish

Copy Editor:
Kate Shoup Welsh

Interior Layout Tech:
Bill Hartman

Cover Designer:
Mike Tanamachi

Indexer:
Sharon Shock

Proofreader:
Heather Urschel

THOMSON

COURSE TECHNOLOGY ™
Professional ■ Technical ■ Reference

Thomson Course Technology PTR, a division of Thomson Learning Inc.
25 Thomson Place ■ Boston, MA 02210 ■ http://www.courseptr.com

Acknowledgments

Putting together a book like this is truly a team effort and thanks must first be extended to all the fine people at Thomson Course Technology. In particular I'd like to point out the efforts of Megan Belanger, Kate Welsh, Mark Abdelnour, and Stacy Hiquet for bringing this project to life.

Also, thanks to the following people who contributed material for the book: Joe Shields, Richard Lent, Neil Steinberg, David Brown, Eric Blumrich, Dermot O'Connor, and Evan Spiridellis.

Finally, thanks to my wife, my son, and the rest of my family for their constant source of inspiration and love.

About the Author

Eric Grebler is an IT professional, author, and certified trainer who has demystified the world of computers for thousands of people. Eric has written books on a wide range of technical topics, including desktop publishing, audio sequencing, graphics, and operating systems.

Contents

Flash Animation for Teens

Introduction

Welcome and congratulations on purchasing *Flash Animation for Teens*. If you are standing in a bookstore or reading this introduction online, what are you waiting for? Check out and let's dive right in to learning about Flash.

I'm no mind reader. In fact, I have no fantastic psychic abilities. But I'm going to take a few guesses to see if I know who you are. You may actually be a teenager who is interested in getting started in Flash animation and is looking for a great resource to get started. If so, you've come to the right place. You may alternatively be the parent of a teenager or young adult who is looking for a good resource for his or her child to start Flash animation. Once again, if so, you've come to the right place. My last guess is that you may not be a teenager or the parent of a teenager at all. You may just be someone who is interested in getting into Flash animation and is looking for a great resource for beginners that isn't intimidating and won't lose you in a wilderness of heavy technical jargon and confusing instructions. Don't let the title of this book restrict you from diving right in. The truth is, this book is specifically designed for *anyone* who is interested in starting the journey to learning about Flash animation, and there is absolutely no experience necessary.

The Goal of the Book

If you've ever taken a karate class, you know that there are several different-color belts you need to earn before you become a black belt. And even when you *do* become a black belt, there are different degrees of black belt that set apart your level of expertise. To become a 10th degree black belt, for example, you need to have passed 17 levels. Using the karate analogy, this book will bring you up to about 10 of the 17 levels of Flash. The goal is to give you a solid foundation in Flash, to get you to a point where you are comfortable creating animations and experimenting on your own. You won't be an expert when you finish this book; expertise takes a lot of time and, most of all, practice. But you will be well on your way. This book is meant for those who have little or no experience in Flash; as a result, several aspects of the program are left out on purpose because they are too advanced for this type of book.

How to Use This Book

Using this book involves a three-step process:

1. Flip page.
2. Read page.
3. Repeat steps 1 and 2.

> People use Flash for many different types of animations, including games, web sites, stand-alone applications, and cartoons. Although this book will teach you techniques that you can apply to all those types of animations, when you are finished you may want to explore resources that tackle specific uses for Flash. Some of those resources are discussed in Chapter 11, "Help If You Need It."

Not very difficult is it? I'm obviously being a little facetious, but my point is that it is a good idea to start at the beginning of the book and follow it chapter by chapter without skipping any chapters or sections along the way. That's because most of the chapters in this book build on the ones before it, and you might get stuck when trying to accomplish a particular task if you haven't read the chapters before it. After you've gone through the book once, feel free to jump to any section as a refresher or use the index or table of contents to find information on a particular topic.

Mac Versus PC

The instructions and screen captures used in this book are given from the PC perspective, but almost all the information and instructions also apply to Macs. The biggest exception is in the use of keyboard shortcuts, but the fix is quite simple. Most keyboard shortcuts on a PC involve the use of the Ctrl key. In almost every case, references to the Ctrl key on the PC can simply be replaced with the Command key on the Mac. For example, if a keyboard shortcut is listed as Ctrl+C (that is, hold down the Ctrl key and press the C key), the equivalent on the Mac would be Command+C (hold down the Command key and press the C key). If at any point a keyboard shortcut does not work for you on the Mac, you can see a full list of appropriate shortcuts by opening the Edit menu and choosing Keyboard Shortcuts. This opens a dialog box that displays all the commands in the program; simply click a command to see what its keyboard shortcut is. If you like, you can even assign a new shortcut for that command.

Version

The instructions in this book were designed for the latest version of Flash at the time of publishing, which is Flash 8. That being said, if you have a previous version (or a future version, for that matter) you will probably be able to accomplish most of the tasks as set out in this book. Typically, the software doesn't change *that* dramatically from version to version, but in the event that one of the steps in this book does not work in your version of Flash, consult the help documentation (see Chapter 11 for information on getting help) to see if there is an alternate way of performing the task.

Pro Files

In most books, you get the instructions and opinions from just one person: the author. This book has an added bonus of views and opinions from several Flash pros. Throughout the book, you'll find "Pro Files," which are interviews with professionals in different roles who use Flash as part of their jobs. These Pro Files are meant to give you insight into the different ways in which Flash can be used and to provide you with tips from people in a variety of industries.

chapter 1
The Not-So-Boring Animation Intro

I f you're interested in diving right into learning about Flash and using it to create animations, then by all means skip this chapter and move on to the next. No, you don't need to re-read that last sentence; I am indeed giving you a pass if you want it. But if you're new to Flash, and I'm guessing many of you are, then you might want to stick around and read this chapter. Here I'll spend just a little bit of time getting you up to speed on what an animation is, how it works, and what components comprise a good animation. I promise I'll keep things short and sweet so you can get down to the business of learning Flash in the next chapter.

What Are Animations?

If you asked 10 different "experts" what an animation is, you'd most likely get 10 different answers. Why the discrepancy? Because animations come in so many different forms. *My* definition of an animation is that it is a technique used to create the illusion of movement in still images by making changes on different frames over time.

Odds are, when you think of the word animation, the first thing that comes to mind is one of your favorite cartoons like *The Family Guy* or *The Simpsons*, or a movie like *Finding Nemo* or *Shrek*. Although it's true that all of those cartoons use animation, the tools used to create those masterpieces are a little different from the ones I'll be discussing here. In this book, when I talk about animations, I'll specifically be discussing animations that have been created using Flash. Flash animations are primarily used on web sites, but can also be used as standalone files that you can share with others. Flash animations are usually short in length—typically a few seconds up to a minute—and unlike your favorite cartoon TV shows or movies, they don't require a team of individuals to create them. You can usually create some impressive animations on your own.

How an Animation Works

I'm guessing that at some point in your life, you've created a flipbook cartoon. If you haven't, creating one is quite simple. Using a notebook containing at least a few pages, draw an image in the bottom-right corner of the first page. On the next page, draw the same image, but make it just a little bit different from the image on the first page. The difference might be its position, its size, or a change in some other attribute like color, texture, or shape. Repeat this step on several other pages, continuing to change the image's attributes on each one. When you finish, quickly flip through the pages; it will appear as though your image is animated.

That's pretty much how an animation works in Flash. In Flash, the equivalent of each page of the flipbook is called a *frame*. When the animation is played, each frame is shown onscreen for a split second. Because the frames are shown so quickly, you can't really tell one from another, but as the frames appear on the screen, they produce an animation.

Figure 1.1 illustrates how you create the illusion of movement in an animation by changing the look of the character from frame to frame. Notice how something minor changes in each frame: the turtle's legs, its arms, its head, the location of the plant, and the position of the clouds all change in each frame. If you were to quickly display each of these frames individually, it would appear as if the turtle was walking.

 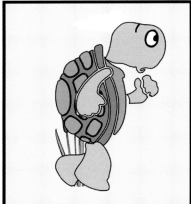 

Figure 1.1 By moving in successive frames the position of the turtle's legs, arms, and head, and the location of the plant and cloud in the background, you can create the illusion of movement when the animation is played.

What Is Flash?

You can think of Flash as two different programs in one. On the one hand, Flash is a drawing and painting program that enables you to create just about any character, background, or object that you can dream up. On the other hand, Flash lets you animate the drawings that you create by providing you with not only the ability to draw on different frames, but also to use a variety of tools to help you create the animations from frame to frame. Chapter 2, "Taking the Tour," explores the different parts of the screen that you'll see when you run Flash, and the rest of the book covers the various tools and techniques that Flash provides to enable you to create your own animated masterpieces.

Planning Your Animation

I used to teach a class called "Speak at Your Peak—Effective Presentation Skills." One of the fundamentals I'd impart to the class was to remember the 7Ps: Prior, Proper Preparation Prevents Poor Performance by the Presenter. So what does this have to do with you? The point is that planning in advance will make all the difference in the world when it comes to creating animations—or just about anything else, for that matter. When building a house, a contractor doesn't just buy some wood and start hammering away; he or she follows a detailed plan that has been outlined by an architect. The same holds true in creating your animations. If you just sit down in front of the computer and start trying to create an animation in Flash without a proper plan, you will get frustrated very quickly, and chances are things won't turn out quite as you hoped. When planning your animation, you'll want to keep the following points in mind.

Your Audience

Think about who the audience for your animation will be, and then take that into consideration when designing and creating your animation. An animation designed for young children is certainly going to have different components than one designed for teenagers.

The Story Line

Even in the simplest animations, *something* happens. This something—the event or events that occur in your animation—is called the *story line*. As a Flash animator, you should establish the story line for your animation by writing it down. The story line is made up of two components: plot and characters.

Plot

Just like in a novel, the *plot* of an animation relates to the events that happen. Your animations, even if they are only a few seconds long, will have a plot. When establishing your story line, you should absolutely write down what you want to happen in your animation.

Characters

In general, one of the big draws of any animation is the character or characters within it. If a character appeals to the audience, they'll be drawn into the animation, and will stay tuned to see what happens. Before you create your characters, you'll want to plan how they will look and sound. Ultimately, the types of characters you create will be limited only by your imagination, but Figure 1.2 shows you some examples that you can use as inspiration. To help in the creative process, ask yourself these questions when planning your characters:

- How tall will the character be?
- How will the character move? Will he or she walk? Run? Crawl? Jump?
- How quickly or slowly will the character move?
- What will the character wear?
- Will the character be holding anything?
- What color will the character be?
- Will the character talk?
- What will the character sound like?
- What facial expressions will the character have?
- What special qualities or characteristics will the character have?
- Will the character be derived from a drawing, a photograph, or a combination of both?

Figure 1.2 Here are some examples of different types of characters that can be used in animations.

THE SUM OF THE PARTS

If you want to create realistic movements for your characters, your characters will need to be broken down into different parts. Why? Because when people or animals move, they usually move at specific joints. To see what I mean, stand in front of a mirror and give yourself a wave. Notice that in order to wave, you probably had to bend your arm at your elbow and move your wrist from side to side. In other words, the movement occurs in two places. Because the same principle should apply when you animate your characters, you'll need to create them in parts, typically at specific joints, in order to create realistic looking movement. To see an example, take a look at Figure 1.3. The image on the left is a character, and the pieces on the right show you the parts necessary to animate this character. In Chapter 4, "Drawing, Selecting, and Importing Objects," you'll learn to create the basic shapes necessary to bring your characters to life.

Figure 1.3 You'll need to create the characters for your animations in parts in order to properly animate them.

The Environment

When creating an animation, you are given the responsibility of playing God. You have the ability to create any kind of world that you like. You can choose how the sky will appear, as well as the ground, the trees, the rivers, and the roads. You also get to establish whether it's day or night, overcast or sunny, or whatever you like. The type of world you create will depend on your animation's plot. If it's a deep, dark, mysterious plot, then the world you create should reflect that by featuring dark lighting, having some fog, and being set at night. On the other hand, if you have a lighter plot, then bright lighting, high detail, and happy characters would be most appropriate.

Sounds and Music

It probably goes without saying that you've seen at least one of the *Star Wars* movies. What do you suppose it would be like to watch such a film with the sound turned off? Not only would it be hard to figure out what is going on (especially because you wouldn't be able to hear the dialog), you'd also be missing one other very big component—music, and the emotions it evokes.

Just as music can be used in movies to create a sense of fear, tension, excitement, joy, sadness, and just about any other emotion, so, too, can music in animations add to the story line. When designing your animation, you'll want to decide where and when you want audio to play. Make sure, though, that the audio choices you make complement the animation rather than overshadowing or otherwise distracting from it.

The bottom line? Your animation will be made up of many elements—plot, characters, environment, and audio—and all these elements should tie in with one another.

Storyboarding

After you have written down your ideas in a story line, it is time to create a storyboard. A *storyboard* is a visual representation of the action and characters in your animation. Think of a storyboard as the comic-strip version of your animation. In a storyboard, you draw a rough sketch of how each scene in your animation is to be played out. In most cases, a storyboard is a black-and-white rough drawing with some text that describes the action, as shown in Figure 1.4.

Although creating a storyboard is a good idea, I don't want you to think that you have to necessarily create one for *every* animation you make. They are, however, extremely useful if you're working on long or complex animations.

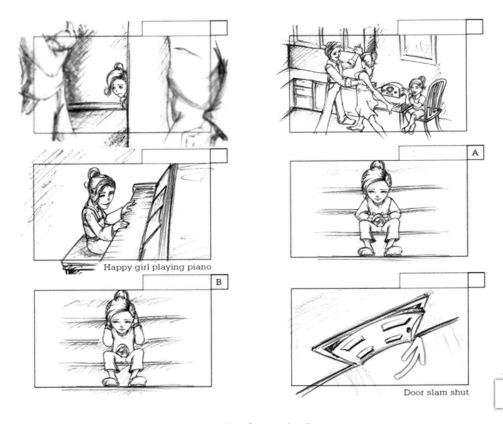

Happy girl playing piano

Door slam shut

Figure 1.4 A storyboard is a visual representation of your animation.

Animating

As I mentioned earlier, an animation occurs when an object in one frame changes in the next. Using Flash, there are literally hundreds of ways to animate an object. There are, however, a handful of basic animation techniques that you'll be using over and over throughout the book:

◆ **Movement.** Repositioning an object from one frame to another is probably the most common form of animation. By moving an object to different locations on different frames you create the illusion of movement, as shown in Figure 1.5.

◆ **Rotation.** Rotating an object from one frame to another creates the illusion that the object is spinning when the animation is played, as shown in Figure 1.6. This technique is very common, especially when animating vehicles.

Figure 1.5 When you change the location of an object from one frame to another, you create the illusion of movement.

Figure 1.6 Rotating an object from frame to frame will make it look as if the object is spinning when the animation is played.

1. The Not-So-Boring Animation Intro

◆ **Size.** When you change the size of an object from one frame to the next, it will appear as though the object is growing or shrinking when the animation is played, as shown in Figure 1.7.

◆ **Color.** You can change the color of an object from frame to frame in order to create some wild-looking effects. Figure 1.8 shows a practical example of changing the color of an object in an animation.

Figure 1.7 Grow or shrink an object by changing its size from one frame to the next.

Figure 1.8 Changing the color of a chameleon as the animation plays is only one example of a practical use for changing the color of an object.

◆ **Shape.** Later in the book, you'll learn more about changing the shape of an object from one frame to another. The technique is called *shape tweening*, and involves creating a start shape and an end shape; Flash automatically creates the frames in between.

◆ **Background.** Another very common technique used in animations is to create the illusion of movement by moving the background rather than the characters or other objects, as shown in Figure 1.9. (Chapter 8, "Putting Your Body in Motion," is devoted to this technique.)

Figure 1.9 You can make an object look as if it is moving by changing the location of the background.

◆ **Combinations.** Most of your animations will contain a combination of effects, as shown in Figure 1.10. That image shows a baseball being hit out of a stadium through a combination of various effects. When this animation is played, the ball appears to get bigger, rotates, and then gets smaller, emulating a baseball being hit in the air and then coming back down again, as seen from a high vantage point.

There you have it—the (hopefully) not-so-boring introduction to animation. The next chapter explores Flash's user interface and introduces some of the program's tools. So what are you waiting for? Turn the page!

1. The Not-So-Boring Animation Intro

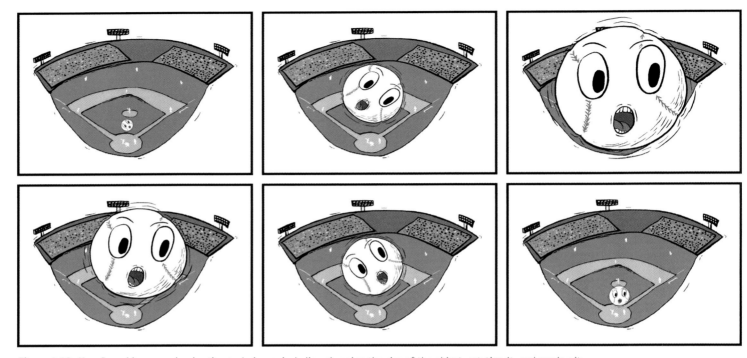

Figure 1.10 Here I combine several animation techniques, including changing the size of the object, rotating it, and moving it.

chapter 2
Taking the Tour

This chapter explores Flash's user interface, *user interface* being a technical term that some computer geek came up with to describe what you see on your screen when you run a program. At first glance, the Flash user interface can seem a little intimidating. There are a whole bunch of tools, windows, sheets, and dialog boxes that may seem really confusing. But don't worry; I'm going to act as your tour guide. Not only are you going to explore the different areas of the screen, you'll also learn how to change the size of screen elements, move them, and save your preferences.

Navigating the Start Page

I'm going to make a big assumption here: If you are reading this book, you've already installed and played around in Flash, or you at least have enough computer savvy to start the program. If not, please don't be offended by my assumption; instead, if you're using Windows, click the Start button, choose All Program, select Macromedia Flash, and choose Macromedia Flash 8 or, if you are using a Mac, open the Applications folder and click the Flash icon. The first thing you should see when you launch the program is the Start page. Think of this page as your launching point for the program. From here you can go off into many different directions. Some of your options include opening files, creating new animations, accessing templates, and getting help. In the following sections you'll explore the options you'll likely use most often.

Starting from Scratch

To create a new blank Flash animation from scratch—something you'll likely do on a regular basis—select the Flash Document option under the Create New column on the Start page, as shown in Figure 2.1.

Opening Files

If you've saved a Flash animation that you worked on previously (I'll cover saving in the next chapter), you can access it by clicking the Open option on the Start page. When you do, Flash launches an Open dialog box, as shown in Figure 2.2; using this dialog box, you can navigate your computer to find the folder and file you need. When you find the file you want to open, either double-click it or click it once to select it and then click the Open button.

> Above the Open link on the Start page, you'll find a list of the last eight documents you have saved. You can click any of these listed files to open the animation.

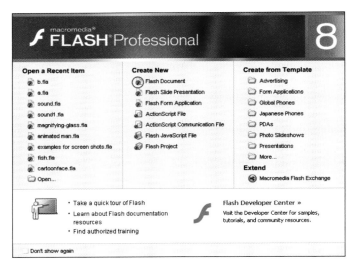

Figure 2.1 Click Flash Document to start a new Flash document from scratch.

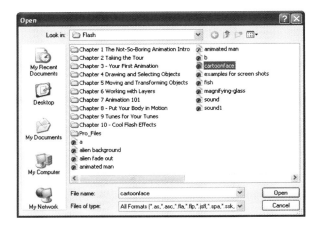

Figure 2.2 Using the Open dialog box, you can navigate your computer to find files you've saved.

Applying Templates

When I think of the word "templates," I usually think of documents that are completely formatted with graphics, standard content, and dummy text that I replace with text of my own. For example, in Microsoft Word, the Professional Letter template features pre-selected margins and fonts, as well as standard openers (Dear Sir or Madam) and salutations (Sincerely), but dummy text for the letterhead and for the body of the letter. Likewise, templates in Flash are essentially documents that enable you to quickly establish the nuts and bolts of your animation—page width, page height, and the like. Unlike templates in Word, however, Flash templates don't have much in the way of pre-fab content. Nonetheless, you can select from a variety of popular document settings for different types of animations. To do so, click any of the template categories on the right side of the Start page and select from the ensuing list of templates that fall within that category. Alternatively, click the More link to open the New from Template dialog box, as shown in Figure 2.3. From here, you can click the appropriate category and then select the template that you want to open.

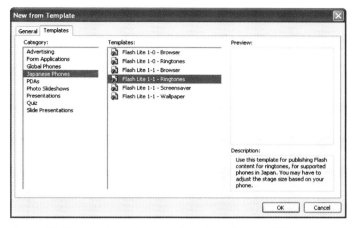

Figure 2.3 You can choose from a variety of templates in different categories.

Taking the Tour

If you'd like to take an animated tour to learn more about Flash, click the Take a Quick tour of Flash link on the Start page. Your default Internet browser will open, and you'll be able to watch a video introducing you to some of the features of the program. To view a different video, click the Video link above the window where the video is playing (see Figure 2.4) and select the desired video. (Keep in mind that because Internet sites are evolving, the videos available may be a little different from what you see here.)

Figure 2.4 You can choose from a variety of videos by hovering over one of the links at the top of the page.

Disabling the Start Page

Not everybody likes the Start page. In fact, many people prefer just to have the program open with a new blank document. If you're not wild about using the Start page, click the Don't Show Again checkbox, shown in Figure 2.5. This places a checkmark in the checkbox and launches a dialog box with instructions on how to re-enable the Start page if you change your mind. Click OK; the next time you start Flash, a new blank document will appear in place of the Start page.

If, after you disable the Start page, you decide you really miss it, you can get it back by opening the Edit menu and choosing Preferences. In the dialog box that appears, shown in Figure 2.6, ensure that the General option is selected in the Category list on the left side, open the On Launch drop-down list, and choose Show Start Page. (Alternatively, select any one of the other menu options.)

Figure 2.5 Disable the Start page by checking this option.

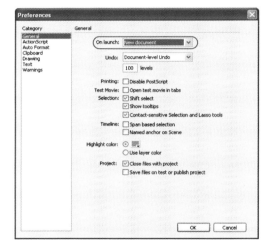

Figure 2.6 You can choose one of several actions to take place when the program launches.

Navigating the Menu Bar

If you've ever used any computer program during your life, and I'm guessing you have, then you are probably familiar with the menu bar. The menu bar provides access to most of the commands within the program. Each word on the menu bar represents a menu that contains a list of commands (see Figure 2.7). To access a menu, simply click on the word in the menu bar; you can then choose a command from the open menu to execute it.

When you expand the menu, you may notice that next to certain command names are letters or symbols. Here is what these letters and symbols mean:

◆ **Letters.** Any letters or numbers next to a command represent the keyboard shortcut you can use to execute that command (see Figure 2.8).

◆ **Triangle.** If a command has a triangle beside it, it means that when you hover over that command with your mouse, a sub-menu of options will appear (see Figure 2.9).

◆ **Three dots.** If a command has three dots beside it, it means that a dialog box will appear when you click the command (see Figure 2.10).

◆ **Checkmark.** If a command has a checkmark beside it, it means that the option is currently selected (see Figure 2.11).

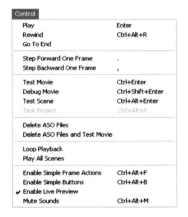

Figure 2.7 You can access the commands of the program by clicking a menu name.

Figure 2.8 The keyboard shortcut for the Find Next command is the F3 key.

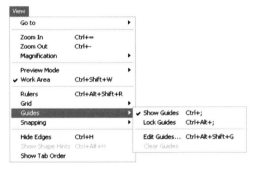

Figure 2.9 Hovering over a triangle expands the menu.

Figure 2.10 Three dots next to a command indicate that a dialog box will open when this command is clicked.

Figure 2.11 A checkmark indicates that the option is selected.

2. Taking the Tour

Using the Timeline

If you recall from the last chapter, an animation is made up of different frames, each displayed for a split second, one after another. In Flash, the *Timeline* (see Figure 2.12) is the control center for these frames. It allows you to manage your frames, control layers, and establish how information is displayed on the Stage.

> Before you begin this section, I urge you to open a blank new document in Flash so that you'll be able to put this discussion in some sort of context.

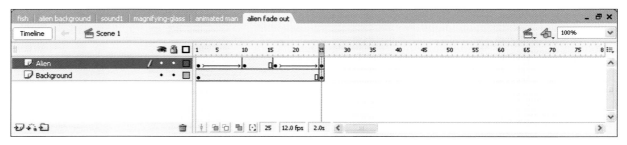

Figure 2.12 The Timeline allows you to control frames and layers.

Navigating the Timeline

The Timeline is made up of two main sections: the Layers area on the left and the Frames section on the right.

The Layers Area

Chapter 6, "Working with Layers," covers layers in detail. For now, you just need to know that by default, when you create an animation, one layer is automatically added on which you can render your objects. This provides you with a way to organize the objects that you include in your animation. You control the various layers in your animation in the Layers area on the Timeline, as shown in Figure 2.13. Notice the icons and colors shown in the Layers area; each of these represents a different layer option.

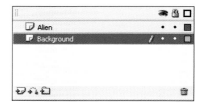

Figure 2.13 The Layers area in the Timeline.

The Frames Area

To the right of each layer name in the Layers area is a series of rectangles. These rectangles are in the Frames area of the Timeline, and each one represents a frame in your animation. When creating your animations, you'll notice that all sorts of little symbols will appear in the Frames area. Here's what most of those symbols (or lack thereof) mean:

◆ **Nothing.** If there is no symbol in a selected rectangle, it means that there is no frame (see Figure 2.14).

◆ **Empty circle.** An empty circle represents an empty keyframe (see Figure 2.15). In a nutshell, a *keyframe* is a frame in which something—for example, an object's position, size, color, or some other attribute—changes. You'll learn all about keyframes in Chapter 7, "Animation 101."

◆ **Solid circle.** A solid circle indicates that the frame is a keyframe (see Figure 2.16).

◆ **Empty rectangle.** An empty rectangle denotes the last empty frame in a layer (see Figure 2.17).

◆ **Arrow.** An arrow denotes the presence of a tween (see Figure 2.18). *Tweening*, short for "in between," is a feature in Flash in which you create the start and end objects and Flash creates the animated frames in between. You'll learn more about tweening in Chapter 7.

◆ **Dashes.** Dashes indicate that a tween has been broken (see Figure 2.19).

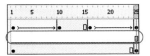

Figure 2.14 A blank rectangle indicates that there is no frame.

Figure 2.15 An empty keyframe.

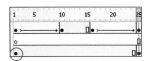

Figure 2.16 A keyframe that contains an object.

Figure 2.17 The last empty frame on a layer.

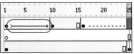

Figure 2.18 A tween is represented by an arrow.

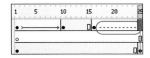

Figure 2.19 Dashes indicate a broken tween.

2. Taking the Tour

17

Other Timeline Features

In addition to the Layers area and the Frames section, the Timeline features all sorts of other points of interest:

◆ **Timeline header.** This is the part of the Timeline that looks like a ruler, as shown in Figure 2.20. The numbers in the Timeline header represent the frame number. For example, the number 10 represents the 10th frame.

◆ **Playhead.** The playhead is the red box in the Timeline header. It indicates the frame that is currently being displayed on the Stage. You can drag the playhead (see Figure 2.21) back and forth on the Timeline header to change which frame is being displayed.

◆ **Indicators.** Notice the boxes at the bottom of the Timeline (see Figure 2.22). Going from left to right, the first box contains the frame number of the selected frame, the next contains the speed of your animation in frames per second (fps), and the last indicates how much time has elapsed in your animation up to the current point. You'll learn more about each of these indicators in Chapter 7.

◆ **Onion Skin options.** Flash's Onion Skin feature enables you to see more than one frame at a time. I'll discuss Onion Skin in Chapter 7; for now, just know that this is where you find the buttons to control this feature (see Figure 2.23).

Figure 2.20 The Timeline header displays the frame numbers.

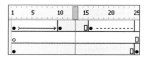

Figure 2.21 Drag the playhead to change which frame is displayed.

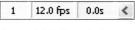

Figure 2.22 These indicators provide you with information about your animation.

Figure 2.23
The Onion Skin feature buttons.

Setting Timeline Options

Unfortunately, unless you have two different monitors, it's difficult to see a lot of the Stage (discussed in the next section) because the Timeline can take up quite a bit of space. On the flip side, if you're working with several layers, it can be difficult to see them all in the Timeline. Fortunately, Flash lets you resize, reposition, and even hide the Timeline as you see fit.

Resizing the Timeline

Depending on the number of layers you've created, you may find it handy to increase or decrease the size of the Timeline to view or hide the layers. Here's how:

1. Position the mouse pointer over the bottom edge of the Timeline. You'll know you're in the right place when the mouse pointer changes to a double-sided arrow, as shown in Figure 2.24.
2. Click and drag up or down to decrease or increase the size of the Timeline, respectively. When you release the mouse button, the Timeline will be resized, as shown in Figure 2.25.

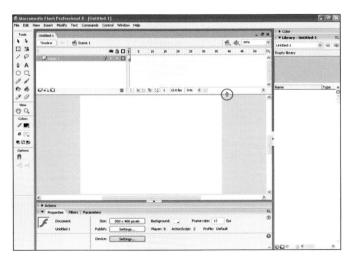

Figure 2.24 You're in the right spot to resize the Timeline when your mouse pointer turns into a double-sided arrow.

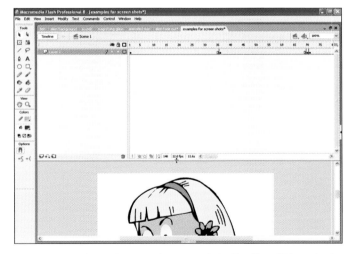

Figure 2.25 Release the mouse button, and the Timeline will be resized.

2. Taking the Tour

Repositioning the Timeline

By default, the Timeline is docked at the top of the window. If you'd prefer to have it elsewhere, you can move it to any other side of the screen, or leave it to float in its own separate window. Here's how:

1. Position the mouse pointer over the two short vertical bars at the top left of the Timeline. You'll know you're in the right place when the mouse pointer turns into a four-sided arrow, as shown in Figure 2.26.

2. Click and drag the Timeline to a new location. As you drag, you'll notice that an outline appears, enabling you to preview the Timeline's position, as shown in Figure 2.27. If you move the Timeline to any of the edges of the screen, it will be docked to that edge; otherwise, it will be left floating.

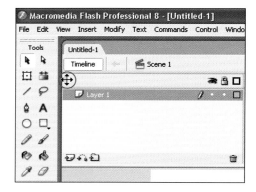

Figure 2.26 The mouse pointer turns into a four-sided arrow when you're in the correct spot.

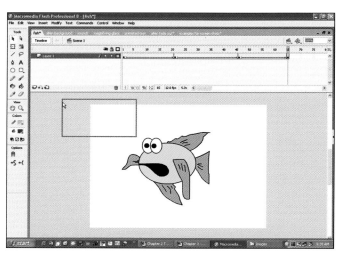

Figure 2.27 As you move the Timeline, an outline will appear, indicating the Timeline's position.

Hiding the Timeline

At the top left of the Timeline, you'll notice a Timeline button (see Figure 2.28). Click this button to hide or show the Timeline.

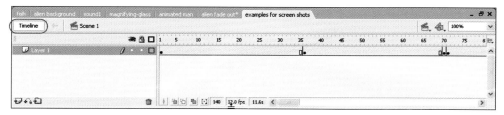

Figure 2.28 Click the Timeline button to hide or show the Timeline.

The Stage

The *Stage* (see Figure 2.29) is the area of the screen where you do all your drawing. The Stage represents one frame of your animation. The main thing that you should know about the Stage is that anything that appears on it will appear in your animation. Compare Figure 2.30 with Figure 2.31; the objects that are on the Stage will appear in the final animation, while those off the Stage will not.

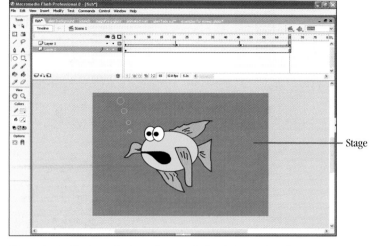

Stage

Figure 2.29 The Stage is the main area of the Flash user interface, where you create your objects.

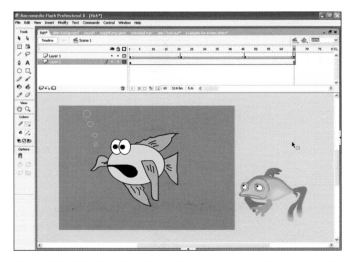

Figure 2.30 Objects off the Stage will not appear when the animation is played.

Figure 2.31 Notice that the fish that was off the Stage does not appear in the final animation.

Using the Tools Panel

Any great artist will tell you that part of creating masterpieces is having the right tools. Flash's Tools panel (see Figure 2.32), on the left side of the screen, contains all the content-creation tools you'll need to create great Flash animations. Using the tools available within the Tools panel, you can create and edit objects, add text, apply fills and outlines, and change the view of the Stage.

Figure 2.32
The Tools panel contains all your content-creation tools.

Just like the Timeline, the Tools panel can be moved to other parts of the screen or be left floating. To move the Tools panel, position your mouse pointer over the two vertical bars at the top of the panel, click, and drag the Tools panel to a new location.

Using the Property Inspector

By default, the Property inspector should appear at the bottom of the screen. (If for some reason the Property inspector is not displayed, you can open it by pressing Ctrl+F3. Likewise, to hide the Property inspector, use this same keyboard shortcut.) The Property inspector is essential to both the creation and animation processes. When you create objects, the Property inspector provides you with information about your objects and allows you to change those properties. Take a look at Figure 2.33. The Property inspector contains information about the size, location, color, outline, and scale of the item on the Stage, and you can change any of these properties. You'll learn more about using the Property inspector to change an object's properties in Chapter 4, "Drawing, Selecting, and Importing Objects." The Property inspector is also handy when creating animations because it allows you to apply and modify various tweening techniques.

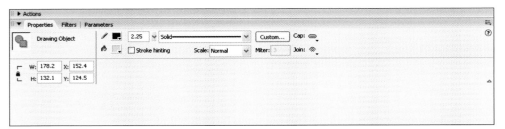

Figure 2.33 The Property inspector contains information about your objects' properties and enables you to change those properties.

22

Using Other Panels, Windows, and Inspectors

In addition to the Timeline, Tools panel and Property inspector, Flash features almost two dozen other windows, panels, and inspectors, each providing different tools that you can use in the creation and animation process. I'll cover many of these tools throughout the book, but feel free to explore and experiment with these windows on your own. Most of them can be accessed from the Window menu (see Figure 2.34). Notice in Figure 2.34 that some of the options listed in the Window menu have checkmarks beside them; this checkmark indicates that the panel, window, or inspector is currently being displayed. To open or close a panel, window, or inspector, simply click it in the Window menu. Most panels, windows, and inspectors will open docked to the right side or at the bottom of the screen, but you can reposition them by placing the mouse pointer over the two vertical lines beside the panel, window, or inspector's name, clicking, and dragging.

Managing the User Interface

One of the problems you may encounter when working with Flash is that if you have multiple documents, panels, and inspectors open, your screen can get quite cluttered. Fortunately, Flash offers a variety of ways to manage these screen elements so that things won't seem so messy. Before you explore those methods, press Ctrl+N, and then click the OK button in the dialog box that appears to open a new document. Repeat this step several times until you have several documents open. Then do the following:

1. Switch from one document to another by clicking the link with the name of the desired document at the top of the screen, as shown in Figure 2.35.

> These links are available only when the window is maximized—that is, it takes up the whole screen. If the window is not maximized, another quick way to switch between documents is to click the Window menu and then choose the desired document's name from the bottom of the menu.

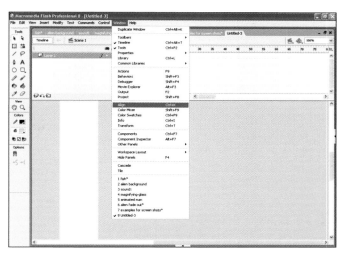

Figure 2.34 You can open and close a panel, window, or inspector by clicking its name in the Window menu.

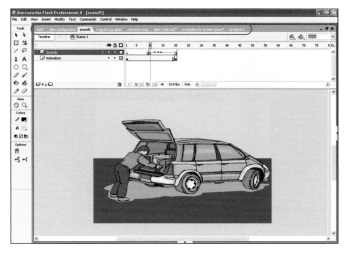

Figure 2.35 Click the document name to switch documents.

2. Taking the Tour

23

2. Expand and collapse every open panel and inspector by clicking the little triangle to the left of each one's name (see Figure 2.36).

3. Move a panel. To begin, position your mouse pointer over the two vertical dotted lines to the left of the panel's name; the mouse pointer will change into a four-sided arrow, as shown in Figure 2.37. Click and drag the panel to a new location on the screen.

4. When a panel is not docked to the side or bottom of the screen (in other words, it is floating), you can make it bigger or smaller to suit your needs. To accomplish this, position the mouse pointer over the blue edge that surrounds the panel. The mouse pointer will turn into a double-sided arrow, as shown in Figure 2.38. You can then click and drag inward or outward to resize the panel. Position the mouse pointer over a horizontal or vertical edge to individually increase or decrease the size horizontally or vertically only; position the mouse pointer over a corner edge to proportionally resize both at once.

Figure 2.36 Click the triangle beside a panel name to expand or collapse the panel.

A quick way to hide all of the panels on the screen so that you can get a better view of your animation is to press the F4 key. You can bring them back by pressing the F4 key again.

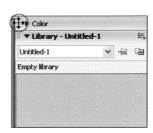

Figure 2.37 You can reposition panels by clicking and dragging on the vertical bars next to a panel's name.

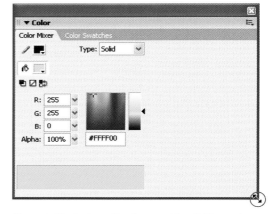

Figure 2.38 Resize a floating panel by clicking and dragging on the panel's edge.

Saving Layouts

One nice feature of Flash is that it has a good memory. For example, Flash will remember the location of any panels you have moved when you close the program so that the next time you open it, the positions of those panels will be the same. Depending on the type of animation you are creating, however, you might want to have a different setup for different types of documents. Also, if you are sharing your computer with others, there is a chance that they will move the panels around to suit *their* needs. Flash allows you to save your current layout so that you can load it at any time, no matter where the panels may have been moved. Here's how:

1. Position and resize the panels until you get the layout you want.

2. Open the Window menu, choose Workspace Layout, and select Save Current.

3. Type a descriptive name for your layout in the dialog box that appears and click OK. The layout is saved.

4. To load a saved layout, open the Window, choose Workspace, and select the name of the layout from the menu that appears.

At any time, you can reset the position of the panels to their default locations by opening the Window menu, choosing Workspace Layout, and selecting Default.

chapter 3
Your First Animation

There are two ways to learn to swim. One is to take lessons, learn the basics, and slowly get into the water. The other is to dive right in and hope for the best. The approach this book takes is a combination of both. In this chapter, I'm going to push you off the pool deck and let you flail a bit to create your first Flash animation. After that, the "swimming" lessons will begin. The lessons in this chapter explore how to set up an animation and how to navigate your Flash documents. It also covers the various methods of frame selection. In the chapters that follow, you'll dive deeper into the other tools Flash has to offer. So put on your life jacket—I'm about to push you in!

Creating Your First Animation

The first animation that you'll create is quite simple. In it, you'll mimic a ball bouncing across your screen. The techniques you use for the actual animation will be discussed throughout the book, so don't worry if you don't quite understand how the animation is created—that's not the point here. The point is to create a quick animation that you can use when learning some of the basics of file management and navigating your documents. To begin, create a new Flash document, as outlined in the previous chapter.

Setting the Size of the Stage

By default, the size of your animation will be 550 pixels (width) by 400 pixels (height). How big you make your animation will depend on where you plan to play the final project. The bigger the animation, the larger its file size, so keep in mind that smaller may be better if you plan to play your animation on the web or send it to others via email. If you want to change the size of the document, simply right-click anywhere on the Stage and choose Document Properties from the menu that appears. This opens the Document Properties dialog box, shown in Figure 3.1. Here you can set the width and height for your animation. For the sake of example, enter a size of 500×500 and then click the OK button.

By default, the unit of measurement for any animation is pixels. If you prefer to work in a different unit, you can select it from the Ruler Units drop-down list in the Document Properties dialog box.

Figure 3.1 You can set the height and width of your animations using this dialog box.

Creating and Animating the Ball

Now that you have your document the size you want, it's time to create and animate your ball. The ball itself will simply be a circle, and it will bounce across the screen. In the next few chapters I'll be going into detail on the techniques you'll use here; for now, just follow these steps to bring your bouncing ball to life:

1. Click the Oval tool in the Tools panel.
2. If it is not already selected, click the Object Drawing button, as shown in Figure 3.2.
3. Click a point to the left of the Stage toward the top of the screen and drag to create an oval, as shown in Figure 3.3. (At this point don't worry about the color of the oval; I cover fills and outlines in the next chapter.)
4. Click frame 10 in layer 1 in the Timeline. The frame will be highlighted in blue, as shown in Figure 3.4.
5. Press F6 on the keyboard to create a keyframe at frame 10. The frame in the Timeline will now contain a dark circle.

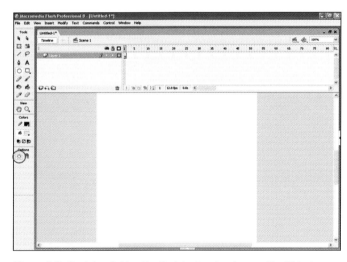

Figure 3.2 Start by clicking the Oval tool and make sure the Object Drawing button is selected.

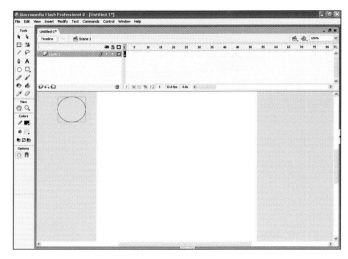

Figure 3.3 Create an oval to the left of the Stage near the top of the screen.

6. Repeat step 5 on frame 20. The Timeline of your animation should now appear the same as the one in Figure 3.5.

7. Click frame 10 in the Timeline, and then click the Selection tool (the button with the black arrow in the top-left corner of the Tools panel).

8. Using the Selection tool, click the circle and drag it to the lower-middle portion of the Stage, as shown in Figure 3.6.

9. Click frame 20 and, using the Selection tool, position the ball to the right of the Stage near the top of the screen, as shown in Figure 3.7.

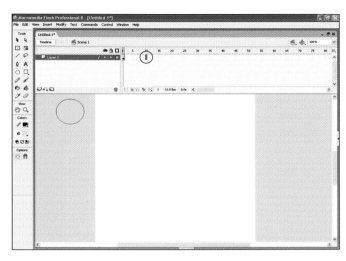

Figure 3.4 Click frame 10 in layer 1 to select it.

Figure 3.5 You should now have a total of three keyframes in the Timeline.

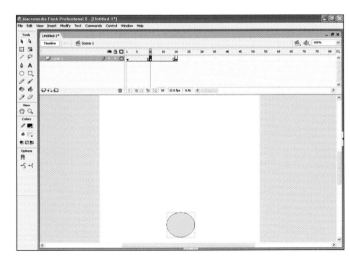

Figure 3.6 Use the Selection tool to move the circle to the lower-middle part of the Stage.

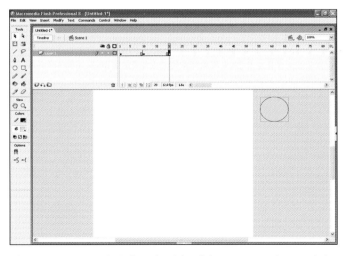

Figure 3.7 Position the ball to the right of the Stage near the top of the screen.

10. Right-click frame 5 in the Timeline and choose Create Motion Tween from the menu that appears (see Figure 3.8). An arrow should now appear in the Timeline between frames 1 and 10.

11. Repeat Step 10 on frame 15. You should now have two arrows in your Timeline, as shown in Figure 3.9.

Ta da! That's it—you've created your animation. Not so hard, right? Now it's time to play it.

Figure 3.8 Right-click frame 5 and choose Create Motion Tween from the menu that appears.

Figure 3.9 You should now have two arrows in the Timeline.

Playing Your Animation

There are really two ways to preview your animation in Flash. The first is to view it directly on the Stage; using this method, the animation plays on the Stage one time. The second is to look at it in a preview window, which, in addition to showing you what your animation will look like when it's played by others outside of Flash, will loop the animation over and over. To play the animation within Flash, simply press the Enter key; press Ctrl+Enter to see the bouncing ball in its own window, as shown in Figure 3.10. As you learned in the last chapter, when an object has been drawn off the Stage, it will no longer be seen by the viewer—which is why, when our ball moves off the Stage, it is no longer visible.

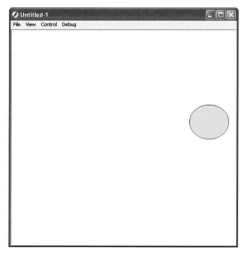

Figure 3.10 Objects off the Stage will not appear when you preview the animation in its own window.

Getting Around Your Documents

Now that you've created an animation, you're ready to spend some time learning how to get around your document. In this section, you'll explore the different zooming and panning options and tools; you can practice these techniques on the animation you just created.

Adjusting the Zoom Level

Although there are many ways to change a document's zoom level, the easiest is probably to use the Zoom tool. This tool allows you to quickly zoom in and out of your animation simply by clicking with the mouse button. Here's how it works:

1. Click the Zoom tool in the Tools panel, as shown in Figure 3.11.

2. At the bottom of the Tools panel is an Options section; when the Zoom tool is selected, the Options section features two magnifying glasses—one with a plus sign and the other with a minus sign. If it is not already selected, click the magnifying glass with the plus sign (see Figure 3.12). Then click your animation to change the zoom level. Continue clicking; each time you do, the zoom level will increase even further.

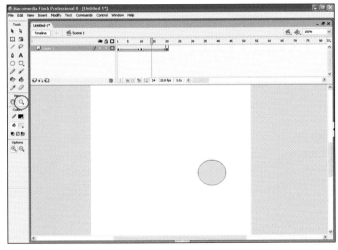

Figure 3.11 Click the Zoom tool to zoom in or out of your document.

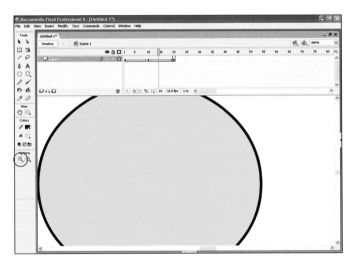

Figure 3.12 Zoom in or out by clicking on the Stage.

3. Your First Animation

29

3. Repeat step 2, except this time click the magnifying glass with the minus sign. When you click your animation, you will zoom out.

4. Another way to change the zoom level is via the Zoom Level drop-down list in the upper-right corner of the screen. Simply click the drop-down arrow and choose one of the zoom options (see Figure 3.13). In addition to the zoom percentages, you'll notice several other options from which you can select:

   ◆ **Fit in Window.** Choose this to change the zoom level so that the frame fits into the window.

   ◆ **Show Frame.** Choose this to change the zoom level so that the entire Stage fits within the window.

   ◆ **Show All.** Choose this to change the zoom level so that all objects can be seen, no matter where they are on the Stage.

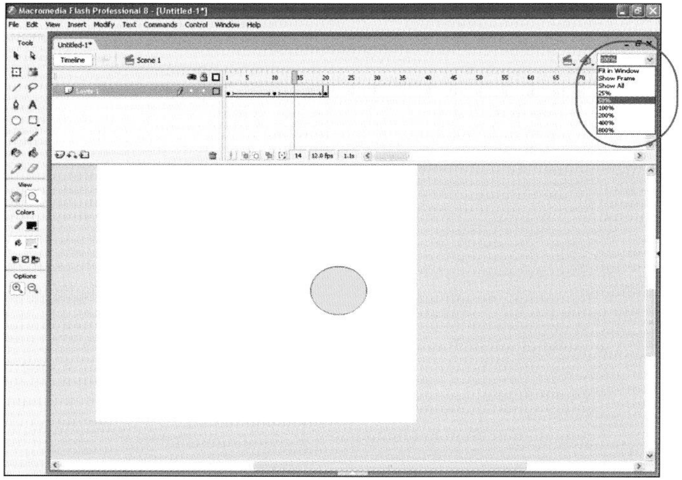

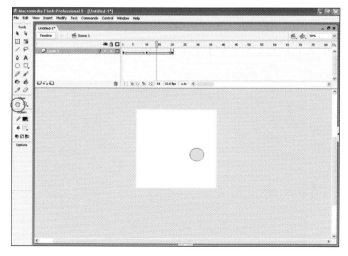

Figure 3.13 There are several zoom options in the Zoom Level drop-down list.

Panning

Panning is a great way to quickly get around within your frame. Using panning, you can move the frame around within the window in order to see the desired area. To use this feature, select the Hand tool (see Figure 3.14), and then click and drag in any direction to move the Stage in the same direction.

Figure 3.14 The Hand tool allows you to pan around the Stage.

Selecting Frames

Later in the book I'll talk about editing frames in your animations. Before you can do any type of frame editing, however, the frames you want to edit must be selected. There are a variety of ways to select frames—two are covered here.

Selecting Frames with the Mouse

Perhaps the easiest way to select frames in your animation is to simply click and drag across the desired frames in your Timeline. As you drag across the frames, the selected frames will be highlighted, as shown in Figure 3.15.

Selecting Frames with the Keyboard

Using both the keyboard and the mouse, you can select contiguous frames (frames that are side by side in the Timeline) or non-contiguous frames (frames that are not together in the Timeline).

1. Start by clicking the first frame that you want to select, as shown in Figure 3.16.

2. Hold down the Shift key and click the last frame that you would like to include in your selection. The first frame you clicked, the last frame you clicked, and all the frames in between will now be selected, as shown in Figure 3.17.

3. Hold down the Ctrl key and click any other frame to add it to your selection, as shown in Figure 3.18. You can repeat this step to continue adding frames to your selection.

4. Without holding down any keys, click any frame. The original selection will be removed; only the frame you just clicked will be selected.

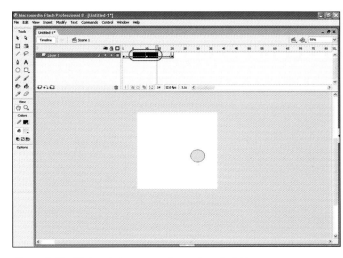

Figure 3.15 Click and drag across frames to select them.

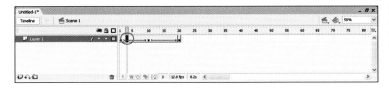

Figure 3.16 Click the first frame that you want to be part of your selection.

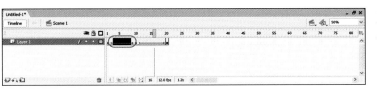

Figure 3.17 The first frame, the last frame, and all the frames in between are selected.

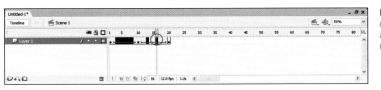

Figure 3.18 Holding down the Ctrl key allows you to select non-contiguous frames.

3. Your First Animation

31

PRO • FILE

Name: Eric Blumrich
Organization: Bushflash.com
URL: http://www.bushflash.com

How did you learn Flash? I'm pretty much self-taught.

How did you get started using Flash? In 1998, I was hired by a multimedia firm in East Orange, New Jersey, and Flash was the hot new technology. Everyone in the office had to learn it, so we all engaged ourselves in our own personal crash-courses in the software. I rebelled at first, but was convinced that it was worth knowing when I learned what it could do with audio.

What feature or tool do you use most often? I only use the basics—opacity/motion keyframing, shape tweens, and basic text animation. If I had to pick a particular "feature" I found most useful in my work, I'd have to say that it's the "stream" audio setting. Being able to hear the sound, frame by frame, is incredibly helpful when it comes to synching animation to music.

What do you like best about Flash? The ability to put together a tremendous amount of material in a package small enough that it's accessible to people using a dial-up connection. There's no other program that can produce a 3–4-minute music video weighing in at under a megabyte.

What sets your animations apart from others? I work mainly in the political realm in my Flash. When I started creating my own work in 2003, other people were doing the same thing, but they tended toward creating stuff that was long on text and short on impact. But the works that have received the most attention are short and visceral, such as "Anniversary" (http://www.bushflash.com/year.html).

On the technical side, what makes my animations different is that I choose with great care the music and pictures that I use. The music is usually obscure stuff that is generally unknown to the American and international public. And the images I choose fill the ENTIRE screen, without any blank areas to either side (an annoying error that everyone else who produces political flash perpetually commits). Sometimes it takes hours to find a single image that conveys the emotion that I want to invoke in the audience.

On a more personal level, what differentiates my work from other Flash in general is that I care—deeply—about my subject matter. A majority of my work concerns the war in Iraq (a conflict that I sincerely hope is over by the time this book sees print). Creating Flash about the horrors of our age, I hope, brings awareness of events and situations that the average person would rather avoid. Hopefully it will cause people to think and consider.

What is the secret to a great animation? Again, you have to care about what you're producing. You can put together a million and one moving widgets and a pounding soundtrack, but unless you have a core concept to build your work around, it's just going to be a muddled mess.

Are there any tips that you can share with the readers about using Flash? Stay away from heavy ActionScript if your goal is to create visual work. This is the MOST IMPORTANT thing to remember. In the early days of Macromedia's development process, they were swayed by those who worked primarily in the "left brain" paradigm and, as a result, came out with successive versions that offered little more than more convoluted script libraries while doing little to improve Flash's core animation tools. While you can spend years and months learning how to create a sine wave out of a single point using ActionScript, that time would be better spent working with the basic animation tools that Flash provides to create something memorable. No one—I repeat, NO ONE—will hire you or feature your work because you can use Java-esque ActionScript expressions and variables to create a screen full of floating bubbles or shifting color patterns. It's unfortunate, but true. If you really want to showcase your talents and leave an impression with the viewer, create a cartoon, a slideshow, or a video feature that shows off your ability to communicate visually.

Are there any animation tips you can share with our readers?

◆ Have the following software available:

    ◆ Photoshop (http://www.adobe.com) for image editing

    ◆ Goldwave (http://www.goldwave.com) for sound editing

    ◆ ImageReady, a Photoshop extension, for image compression

◆ Never rely on the default sound settings in Flash. Always bump the sound quality up to at least 20Kbps (open the File menu, choose Publish Settings, select Flash, choose Audio Stream/Event, click set, Set, and change the Bit Rate/Quality setting) and enable stereo sound. It increases the file size minimally, but enhances the quality of the piece immeasurably.

◆ If you're using a lot of bitmap graphics (JPEGs and GIFs), bump image quality down to 50 percent (open the File menu, choose Publish Settings, select Flash, and change the JPEG Quality setting). If an image is only going to be on the screen for a few frames, the minimal loss in quality won't register with the viewer.

◆ Images for a typical 550×400 Flash movie need only be 320×240 in size. When you bring them into Flash, you can scale them to the screen using the Align tool (Ctrl+K).

◆ ALWAYS use a loader. Even if the viewer has broadband, you'll need to allow buffering. Otherwise, everything will be out of synch.

◆ Frequent http://www.flashkit.com often. This site has thousands upon thousands of open-source FLAs, sound loops, sound effects, and scripts available for downloading and customization.

Do you have any other advice for teens getting started with Flash animations? Give it time. It can be daunting at first. Flash has a ton of features and tools, but the beauty of Flash is that you can pick and choose which elements best suit your creative goals.

Samples

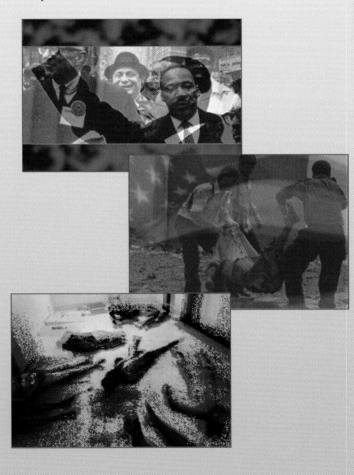

chapter 4
Drawing, Selecting, and Importing Objects

W hat do you call an animation with no characters, colors, backgrounds, or other objects? That's an easy one—nothing! In order to change your animation from nothing into something, you really have only two options: You can create your images from scratch, or you can import images that have already been created. This chapter explores both options. It starts by covering the tools that allow you to create and select your objects, and then it talks about how you can import images and objects that you've either downloaded or received from other people.

Drawing Objects

Imagine a car mechanic who had only one tool—say, a screwdriver—to fix cars. He'd probably have a hard time handling most repairs! If he could do it at all, it would probably take him hours and hours to complete any job because resolving most car issues usually requires a variety of tools. That's why mechanics have toolkits with hundreds of different tools to get the job done right. The same is also true in Flash. The process of creating most images requires a variety of different drawing tools. The good news is that Flash features a Tools panel that is stacked with different implements to help you create just about any image you'd like. So let's dive right in and start creating!

Creating Ovals, Circles, Squares, Rounded Rectangles, Polygons, and Stars

The title of this section includes a lot of different shapes, but that's because the process of creating all of these shapes is pretty much the same. All you have to do is select the type of shape you want to create and then simply click and drag.

Drawing an Oval

Let's start by creating an oval so you can see how it's done:

1. Click the Oval tool. As with most tools in the Tools panel, when you select the Oval tool, it will appear highlighted, and your mouse pointer will change into a cross-hair. Move the mouse around the Stage to specify where you want the oval to begin.

2. Click and drag across the Stage. As you drag, a preview outline of your oval will appear, as shown in Figure 4.1. Without letting go of the mouse button, move the mouse in different directions; the oval will change its shape as you drag.

3. Release the mouse button. An oval will appear on the screen in the default color (see Figure 4.2).

Congratulations! You just created your first shape. Pretty easy, wasn't it? Hopefully this is the first of a long line of shapes that you'll create.

CREATING PERFECT SHAPES

To draw a perfectly symmetrical shape—for example, a circle rather than an oval or a square instead of a rectangle—hold down the Shift key as you drag. Release the mouse button before you let go of the Shift key, and you'll have a perfectly symmetrical shape.

USING UNDO AND REDO

Now that you have created your first oval, it's time to get rid of it. Later in the chapter I'll talk about using the Eraser tool to remove all or part of an object. For now, let's use a feature called Undo—a feature that will quickly become your new best friend. Whenever you create something by accident or make some other mistake, you can use the Undo command to go back a step. To undo your last action on the Stage—in this case, creating the oval—press the Ctrl+Z keyboard shortcut or open the Edit menu and choose Undo. Thanks to Undo, you can make a ton of mistakes, penalty-free; just keep undoing until you reach the point where you made the mistake. If you use the Undo command one too many times, overshooting the mistake you *meant* to undo, you can move forward a step using the Redo command. To access the Redo command, open the Edit menu and choose Redo or press Ctrl+Y.

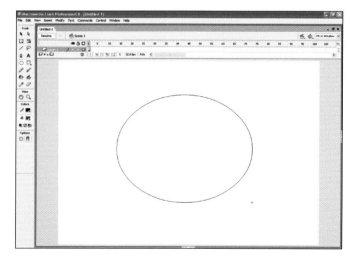

Figure 4.1 As you drag, the shape of the oval will change until you release the mouse button.

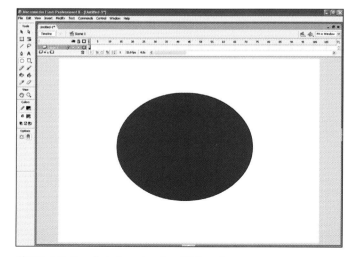

Figure 4.2 Your first shape is a beautiful oval!

Flash Animation for Teens

Creating Rounded Rectangles

Creating a rectangle is just like creating an oval. You simply select the Rectangle tool from the Tools panel, and then click and drag across the Stage. Unlike the Oval tool, however, the Rectangle tool has an additional option: It allows you to create rectangles with curved corners.

If you haven't already done so, remove the oval that you created by pressing Ctrl+Z. Then do the following:

1. Click the Rectangle tool in the Tools panel. Notice that the Options area now offers an option to create a curved rectangle.
2. Click the Set Corner Radius button. (This button looks like a curved line with a little blue triangle attached to it.) A dialog box opens, asking you to enter a value for the radius of the corner.
3. Enter a value for the radius of the corner, as shown in Figure 4.3. This number dictates how round the corner of the rectangle will be—the larger the number, the rounder the corners. After you enter a value, click the OK button; you're now ready to create your curved rectangle.
4. Click and drag across the Stage. As you drag, you'll see a preview of your rounded rectangle; when you release the mouse button, like magic, your rounded rectangle will appear (see Figure 4.4).

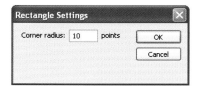

Figure 4.3 The value that you enter for the corner radius determines how round the corners will be.

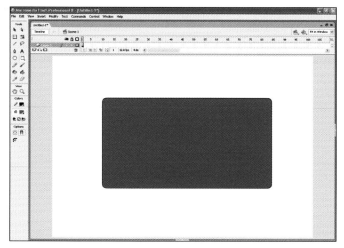

Figure 4.4 This rounded rectangle has a corner radius of 10.

WORKING WITH FILL AND OUTLINE

Every shape that you create in Flash is made up of two different elements: an outline and a fill. By default, an object's outline and fill act as two separate shapes. In other words, the outline and fill aren't attached to one another, and if you alter one, the other remains intact. If you want to attach the outline and the fill of a shape to each other so that a change to one affects the other, you need to select the Object Drawing option button found in the Options section of the Tools panel. It can also be accessed by pressing the letter J on the keyboard. Later in this book, you'll learn how to change the size and color of both the outline and the fill.

Drawing Polygons and Stars

What exactly is a polygon, anyway? According to the dictionary, a polygon is "a closed plane figure bounded by straight sides." Okay, so what does that mean? Simply put, a polygon is a multi-sided shape, where each side is made up of a straight line. Creating a polygon is not really any different from creating any other shape in Flash, but there are a few options that you can set, including the number of sides on the polygon.

To create a polygon, you use the PolyStar tool. Actually, the PolyStar tool has two jobs. Not only can you use it to create polygons, you can also create stars with it. To adjust the PolyStar options, you use the Property inspector.

1. Notice that the button for the Rectangle tool has a little triangle in its bottom-right corner. This indicates that other tools are accessible from this one button. To access the hidden tools, click and hold the Rectangle tool button; a menu listing the additional tools appears (see Figure 4.5). Click the PolyStar Tool option. Now you're set to start making polygons and stars.

2. You could click and drag across the Stage now to create the default polygon, which has five sides. Rather than doing that, however, take a moment to explore some of the options for creating a polygon. To begin, launch the Property inspector if it is not already open at the bottom of your screen by opening the Window menu, choosing Properties, and selecting Properties, or by pressing Ctrl+F3.

3. Click the Options button in the Property inspector, located at the bottom of the screen, to launch the Tool Settings dialog box. This dialog box, shown in Figure 4.6, allows you to set the options for your polygons, including the number of sides and whether the shape will be a polygon or a star.

4. Click the Style drop-down arrow. You'll see two different options: Polygon and Star. Click the Star option. You can now enter the number of sides for the star, as well as the point size, which indicates how "deep" the sides of the stars will be. Figure 4.7 shows three different stars with different point sizes.

5. Click and drag across the Stage. A star is born!

Now that you have set up the PolyStar tool to create star, it will continue creating stars until you change the options again.

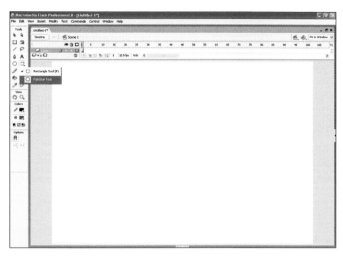

Figure 4.6 This dialog box enables you to control whether a star or polygon is created when you use the PolyStar tool.

Figure 4.5 Click and hold down any button with a little rectangle in the bottom-right corner to access "hidden" tools.

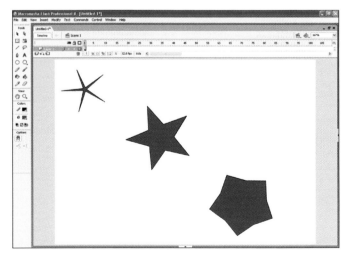

Figure 4.7 The top-left star has a point size of 0.25, the middle star has a point size of 0.5 and the bottom-right star has a point size of 1.0.

Drawing with the Pencil Tool

I know I'm taking a big leap of faith here, but I'm assuming that at some point in your life, you've used a pencil. Assuming that's true, you'll be happy to learn that you use the Pencil tool in Flash much the same way you use a real pencil. The primary exception is that you use the mouse, rather than your hand, to draw.

As you'll see in a moment, Flash actually makes drawing with the Pencil tool *easier* than drawing with a pencil in real life. I'll be honest with you—although I consider myself a graphic designer, I can't draw! Seriously, I couldn't draw my way out of a paper bag. But with Flash, I don't need to. If I draw a rough circle, Flash turns it into a perfect circle. If I draw a rough line, Flash automatically converts it into a straight line. Then again, if I want to just draw roughly, Flash will keep my rough drawings as is.

So let's get drawing with the Pencil tool:

1. Click on the Pencil tool. You can now draw away by clicking and dragging across the Stage. When you release the mouse button, your line will be created.

2. Unlike the shapes you drew earlier, which were filled by default, the shapes you draw with the Pencil tool will have just the outline. To fill an object drawn with this tool, you must ensure that it is closed. To do so, release the mouse button at the same point where you began drawing the shape. Figure 4.8 shows you the difference between a closed and open pencil drawing.

3. Now let's explore the Pencil tool options that will make your life a lot easier. In the Options section, you'll notice a button with a curvy line and a black triangle in the bottom-right corner; this triangle indicates that you can access multiple options from this button. Click and hold down on the button and you'll see the three options: Straighten, Smooth, and Ink (see Figure 4.9). To begin, select Straighten.

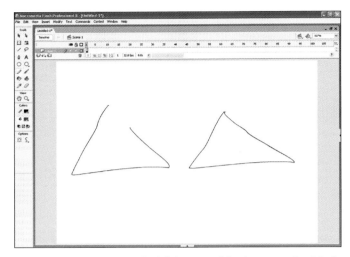

Figure 4.8 The triangle on the left is open, while the one on the right is closed. Only the closed triangle can be filled with a color.

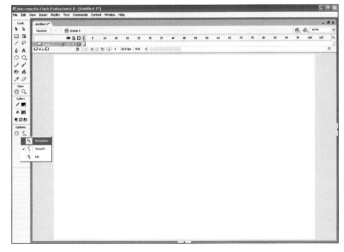

Figure 4.9 The three different Pencil drawing options are Straighten, Smooth, and Ink.

4. Have you ever tried to draw a perfectly straight line on paper? It's pretty tough! Take things a step further and try to draw a rectangle or triangle with perfectly straight lines—it's even more difficult. To make your life easier, the Straighten option turns your rough drawings into perfectly straight shapes. (Where was this tool during art class?!) To use it, select the Straighten option mentioned in step 3. Then, using the Pencil tool, try to draw a straight line. As you draw, a preview of your rough line will appear (see Figure 4.10); when you release the mouse button, however, your line will be perfectly straight (see Figure 4.11).

5. Next, use the Pencil tool to draw a rough triangle. When you release the mouse button, the triangle will be nice and straight, as shown in Figure 4.12.

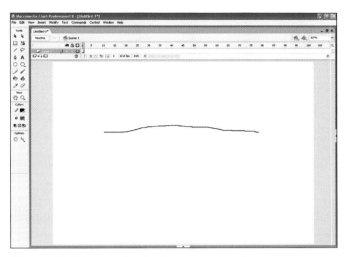

Figure 4.10 This is how the line looks as you draw it.

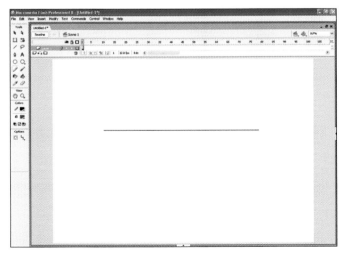

Figure 4.11 When you release the mouse button, the line is automatically straightened.

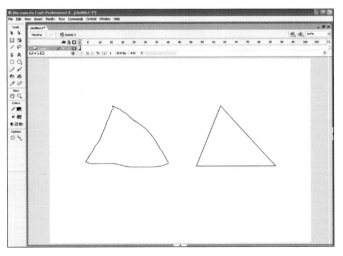

Figure 4.12 The triangle on the left was drawn freehand, and the one on the right was drawn using the Straighten option.

6. Drawing with a mouse can be difficult, because any shakes in your hand will be amplified and will show up in your drawing. To rectify this, select the Smooth option. To begin, click the Smooth option mentioned in step 3, and then click and drag to create a shape or line. When you release the mouse button, the line or shape you drew will be smooth, as shown in Figure 4.13.

7. Next, choose the Ink option mentioned in step 3 and draw a square. Does it seem like there isn't much difference between the Smooth and Ink options? Guess what—you're right! The difference between the two, which is very subtle, is that the Ink feature does not modify your lines. Figure 4.14 shows you the difference between the three drawing options.

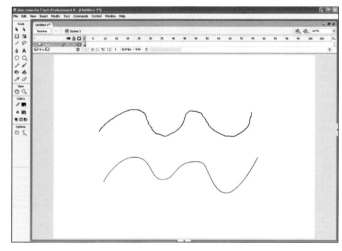

Figure 4.13 The top line is how the pencil drawing looks before smoothing, and the bottom one shows the results of using the Smooth option.

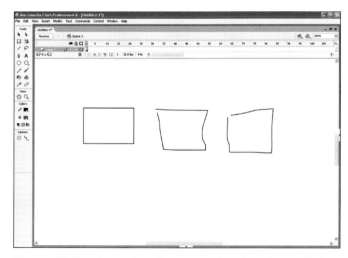

Figure 4.14 From left to right, these squares have been drawn with the Straighten option, the Smooth option, and the Ink option.

Exploring Pencil Properties

By changing the properties of the Pencil tool, you can change the thickness of your lines, their shape, their color, their smoothness, and other options.

1. If you don't already have it open, launch the Property inspector by opening the Window menu, choosing Properties, and selecting Properties, or by pressing Ctrl+F3.

2. The Property inspector opens at the bottom of the screen, displaying a variety of options for changing the properties of your pencil drawing (see Figure 4.15). Click any of the drop-down arrows to view menus with options enabling you to adjust the color, size, or style of the line. To see a variety of other options for the Pencil tool, click the Custom button.

3. Click and drag across the Stage. As you drag, a preview of the line appears; when you release the mouse button, you'll see your line or drawing with the new properties you selected.

If you want to change the properties of a line or shape *after* you've drawn it, you must select it first and then adjust the settings in the Property inspector. I'll talk about selecting objects a little later in this chapter.

Drawing with the Brush Tool

The Brush tool works in much the same way as the Pencil tool, with just a few differences. By default, the Pencil tool creates an outline, while the Brush tool creates a shape with its own outline and fill. Here's how it works:

1. Click the Brush tool, which is right beside the Pencil tool. The cursor will turn into a dot.

2. Click the Fill Color drop-down arrow (the one with a paint-can icon). A palette of colors from which you can choose will appear, as shown in Figure 4.16; go ahead and click on any color for your brush. This will be the fill color for your shape. You can just as easily change the color of the outline by selecting a color from the Stroke Color palette, which is just above the Fill Color palette.

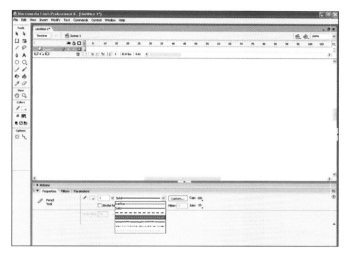

Figure 4.15 The Property inspector provides you with a variety of options, including stroke color, size, and style.

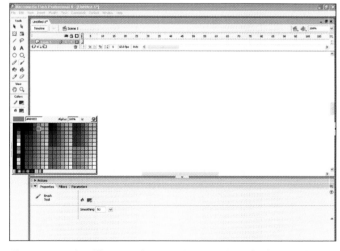

Figure 4.16 The Fill Color palette provides a variety of color swatches from which you can select.

3. Click the Brush Size drop-down arrow to bring up a menu of different sizes for your brush, displayed as little circles, as shown in Figure 4.17. Click the size of brush that you would like to use for your drawing.

4. Click the Brush Shape drop-down arrow to see a menu of different shapes for the head of your brush. Click any one of these shapes to select it, and then click and drag across the Stage to paint, as shown in Figure 4.18.

Figure 4.17 The Brush Size drop-down list provides a variety of brush sizes from which you can select.

Figure 4.18 After you select a shape for your brush, you can click and drag on the Stage to draw.

Using Brush Modes

Flash provides five different brush modes to control how your brush strokes react with other objects on the Stage. To access these brush modes, click the Brush Modes drop-down arrow in the Options section; a menu of options from which you can select will appear. These options, illustrated in Figure 4.19, include the following:

◆ **Paint Normal.** In this brush mode, the stroke will paint over everything.

◆ **Paint Fills.** In this mode, only items that have fills and empty areas will be painted. In other words, you can't paint over outlines with this mode.

◆ **Paint Behind.** In this mode, the brush stroke paints behind everything else on the Stage.

◆ **Paint Selection.** In this mode, only areas that are selected will be painted. (You'll learning about creating selections later in this chapter.)

◆ **Paint Inside.** In this mode, you will paint only the fill of the object in which you started painting.

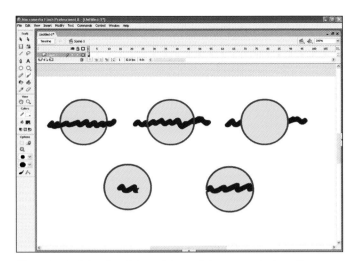

Figure 4.19 Going from left to right, and then top to bottom, these circles show the Normal, Fills, Behind, Selection, and Inside brush modes.

Using the Line Tool

It doesn't take a rocket scientist to figure out what the Line tool does—it draws lines. As with other tools, you can change the size, color, and style of the line. In order to change these options, you need to have the Property inspector displayed; if it's not already, press Ctrl+F3. Then do the following:

1. Click the Line tool in the Tools panel.
2. Adjust the size, shape, and color of your line in the Property inspector.
3. Click and drag across the Stage; lo and behold, when you release the mouse button, there's your line (see Figure 4.21).

USING THE PRESSURE AND TILT OPTIONS

If you have a tablet attached to your computer, you may have noticed two buttons at the very bottom of the Options section (see Figure 4.20). (A *tablet* is a piece of computer hardware that enables you to use a pen rather than a mouse to control the movement of the cursor.) The button on the left is the Pressure button; when it is selected, the harder you press the pen on your tablet, the more "ink" will flow onscreen. The button on the right is the Tilt button. If your tablet supports the Tilt option, then selecting it here will enable you to control the flow of "ink" based on the angle of the pen on the tablet.

Figure 4.20 These two buttons are designed specifically for those people using a drawing tablet.

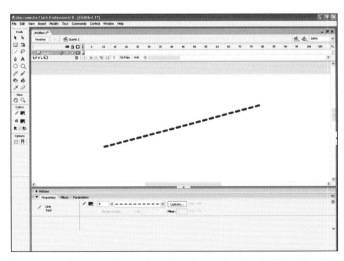

Figure 4.21 You can change the color, size, and style of a line using the Property inspector.

Using the Pen Tool

I'll give you a little warning before you proceed with this section: Using the Pen tool isn't easy—at first. Once you get the hang of it, however, you'll find it to be the most precise drawing tool. This section shows you how to use the Pen tool in a variety of ways, starting slow and working your way to more complex drawings.

1. Select the Pen tool and click once on the Stage. As shown in Figure 4.22, a little green circle will appear at the point where you clicked.

2. Move the mouse pointer to the left or right of the circle and click again. A line appears, extending from the point of your first click to the current point, as shown in Figure 4.23.

3. Now move your mouse pointer to any other location on the Stage and click. Your line continues to this new point.

4. Finally, click at the point where you started. The lines you just created will form the outline of a shape that closes when you click at the original location (see Figure 4.24). The shape you created will be filled with the default color.

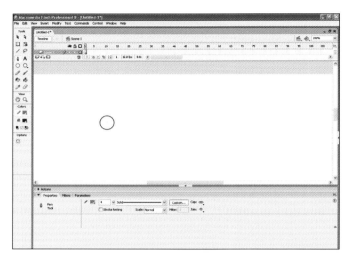

Figure 4.22 It's hard to see, but a little green circle appears when you click the Stage with the Pen tool.

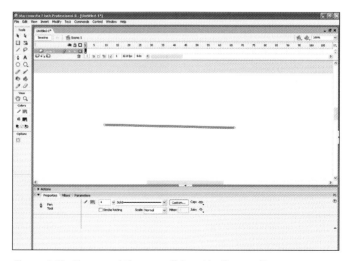

Figure 4.23 The second time you click on the Stage, a line appears, connecting the first point to the second point.

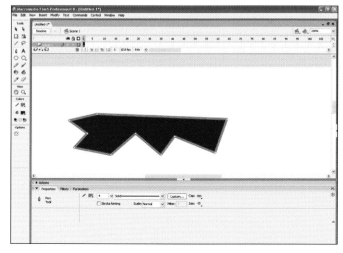

Figure 4.24 When you click at the point where you started, the shape closes and is filled with the default fill color.

Flash Animation for Teens

Creating Curves with the Pen Tool

In the last section, you created a shape using the Pen tool—a job that is probably a lot easier with the Line or Brush tool. The main purpose of the Pen tool is to create lines with curves, which is what you'll explore here.

1. Select the Pen tool and click once on the Stage. A little green circle will appear at the point where you clicked.

2. Move your mouse pointer to another location on the Stage. This time, rather than just clicking, click and drag—but don't release the mouse button.

3. With the mouse button held down, move the mouse up or down to create a curve. The more dramatic the move, the sharper the curve.

4. Drag left or right to adjust the center point of the curve, as shown in Figure 4.25.

5. As you drag, a preview of the line will be displayed, and when you release the mouse button, the curve itself will appear.

6. To create another curve that is attached to the first, click in another location on the Stage and drag to a point on the initial curve.

Figure 4.25 As you drag left and right or up and down, the center point and the height of the curve change.

Say you're creating a curve with the Pen tool and you want to stop and create a new curve in another location. You have three options. One is to close the shape by clicking at the point where you started—although if you want an open curve, this won't work. The easiest option is to press the Esc key, which ends your curve and lets you start a new curve. Finally, you can simply select a different tool to end the curve.

4. Drawing, Selecting, and Importing Objects

Drawing with the Eraser

I know it sounds funny, because usually you use an eraser to erase things, but you can use Flash's Eraser tool to draw some interesting shapes. For example, you can use the Eraser tool to remove parts of an existing image to create all sorts of cool images. You can also use this tool to touch up existing images.

1. Create an oval anywhere on the Stage. Don't worry about the color or size; you just need a shape to work with.

2. Click the Eraser tool, and then click the drop-down arrow under Options to see a list of different shapes and sizes; click any of the sizes or shapes for the Eraser tool.

3. Click and drag across the shape. As you drag, parts of the shape will be erased, as shown in Figure 4.26.

4. To erase everything on the Stage, double-click on the Eraser tool.

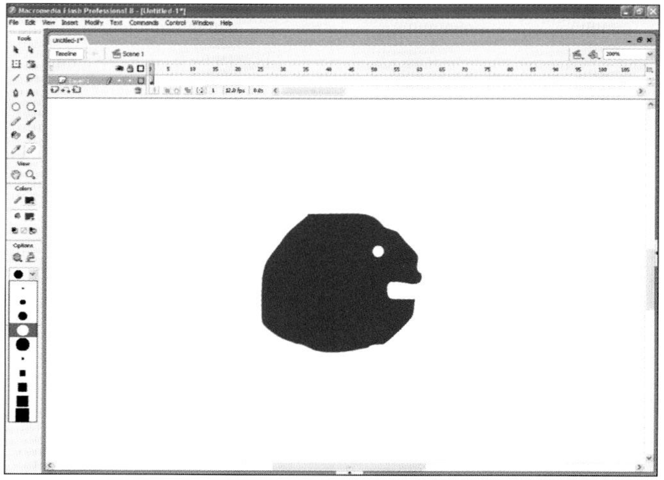

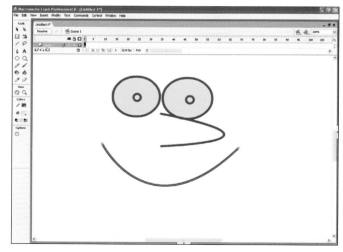

Figure 4.26 You can use the Eraser tool to create all sorts of interesting shapes.

Now You Try

So far, you've learned about quite a few tools. Now it's time to put what you've learned to the test. Using only the tools we've already covered, I want you to try to draw the image you see in Figure 4.27. Don't worry about the color and fill of the face, just concentrate on the shapes. (I'll cover colors in more detail in the next chapter.) If you've tried and succeeded, good for you! If not, don't worry; just follow these steps to get up to speed.

1. Open the Property inspector by pressing Ctrl+F3.

2. Click the Oval tool, and set the line stroke height to 4. If you want to, change the fill and outline color to whatever color you like.

3. Hold down the Shift key and click and drag on the Stage to create a circle in the location shown in Figure 4.28 to create the face's first eye. Repeat this step to create a second eye beside the first, as shown in Figure 4.29.

Figure 4.27 Try to re-create this cartoon face.

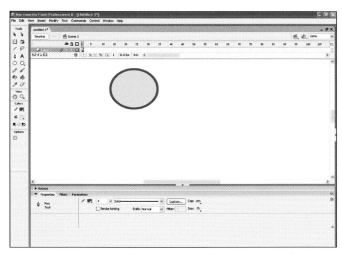

Figure 4.28 Position the first circle in the upper-left portion of the Stage.

4. Repeat step 3 to create eyeballs within the two eyes, as shown in Figure 4.30.

5. Now it's time to create the nose. Select the Pen tool and click once about an inch and a half under the two eyeballs, right between them. A green dot will appear where you clicked.

6. Click between the two eyeballs and drag to the left until the preview of the nose looks like the one in Figure 4.31. When it looks okay, release the mouse button, and your nose is created. (Well, not *your* nose, but the nose of the character you are drawing.) Press the Esc key.

7. Click underneath and to the left of the nose to start the mouth. A green dot will appear.

8. Click to the right of where you clicked in step 7 and drag upward and to the right until the smile looks like the one you see in Figure 4.32. Ta da! You've created the cartoon face. Not exactly a masterpiece, but a good start.

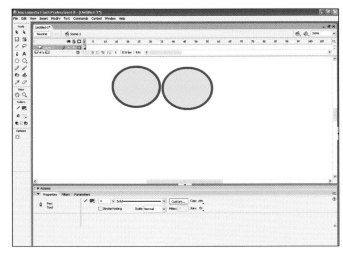

Figure 4.29 Create the second circle just to the right of the first.

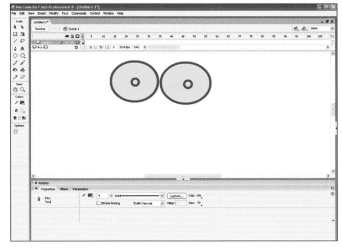

Figure 4.30 Draw two eyeballs in the circles you created.

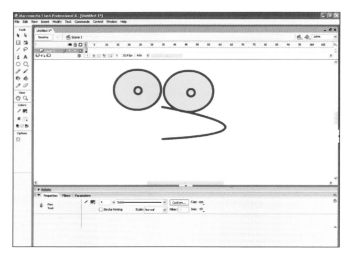

Figure 4.31 The nose should look something like this when you release the mouse button. If it doesn't, press Ctrl+Z and try again.

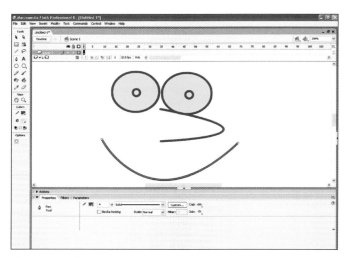

Figure 4.32 The cartoon face should look something like this when you are finished.

Adding Text

Odds are, you'll want to add text to your animations at least part of the time—especially if you are creating Flash animations for use on the Internet. Adding text to your animations is really quite simple; you just click on the Stage with the Text tool and type away! After your text is created, you can change its size, font, color, spacing, style, and other properties.

1. Click the Text tool and then click the Stage. You can now type the desired text. As you type, you'll notice that a box appears around the text.

2. Click anywhere outside the box when you are finished typing.

3. Click the text again with the Text tool. The box around the text will reappear, allowing you to add more text or delete parts of the existing text. To delete text, click and drag across the text to select it (see Figure 4.33) and then press the Delete or Backspace key.

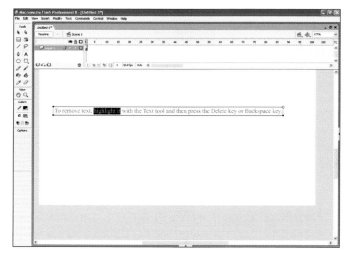

Figure 4.33 To remove text, select it with the Text tool and then press the Delete or Backspace key.

4. To add text, simply click at the point where you would like to insert the new text and begin typing. If you're adding text to existing text, you'll notice that as soon as you reach the edge of the box, a new line will be started. If you don't want to start a new line, simply resize the text box by clicking and dragging one of the box's right-most handles (represented by little black nodes or squares).

Modifying Text Properties

Changing the properties of your text in Flash is similar to changing text in any other program. In addition to changing the properties of text you've already typed, you can establish your text settings beforehand.

1. If the Property inspector is not already displayed, press Ctrl+F3 to open it. It will appear at the bottom of the screen.

2. With the Text tool selected, click and drag across existing text whose properties you want to change. Alternatively click once in a new area and change the text properties before you begin typing.

3. Within the Property inspector, change any of the text properties, including the font, its size, its color, and a variety of other options (see Figure 4.34). You can even add a URL so that when someone clicks the text, he or she will be taken to a specific Internet location.

Selecting Objects

Being able to select objects is of utmost importance in Flash. After you have an object selected, you can perform all sorts of tasks such as color the object, resize it, reshape it, or move it to another location. You can also select multiple objects at once and apply changes to them as a group, all at the same time. This section covers the ways you can make selections in Flash.

Using the Selection Tool

The Selection tool is your primary tool for selecting objects in Flash. As you learned earlier in this chapter, each object is made of a fill and an outline. The Selection tool allows you to select an object's outline, its fill, or both. To do so, you can either create a marquee or click directly on an object or its outline. Follow these steps to get a handle on selecting objects:

1. Start by creating an Oval in the middle of the Stage. When you're finished, click the button for the Selection tool. (The Selection tool is the button in the top-left area of the Tools panel that features a black arrow.)

2. Click once in the middle of the oval to select the oval's fill. When selected, the fill will have a mesh-like appearance, as shown in Figure 4.35.

Figure 4.34 You can change many text attributes within the Property inspector.

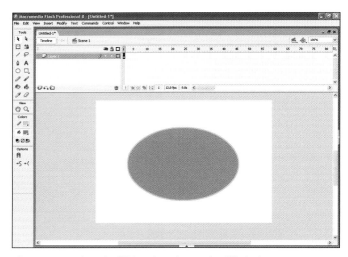

Figure 4.35 When the fill is selected, a mesh of little dots appears over it to indicate the area that is selected.

3. Click any blank area away from the object, either on the Stage or on the gray background, to de-select the oval fill. The mesh will disappear.

4. Click on the oval's outline. As shown in Figure 4.36, the selected outline will assume a mesh-like appearance, indicating that it is selected.

5. Again, click in any blank area of the Stage or screen to de-select the outline.

6. Position the mouse pointer up and to the left of the oval, as shown in Figure 4.37, and then click and drag downward and to the right. As you drag, a *marquee* (black box) will appear, indicating the area that will be selected. Continue dragging until the box completely surrounds the oval and then release the mouse button to select everything within the marquee—in this case, the oval and its outline.

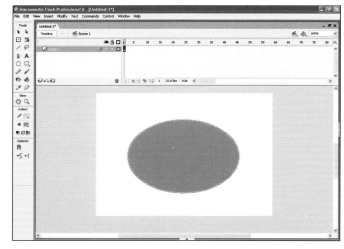

Figure 4.36 It may be a little difficult to see, but the outline of this oval is selected because a mesh appears over the outline.

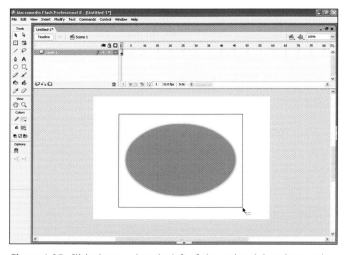

Figure 4.37 Click above and to the left of the oval and drag down and to the right to create a marquee.

7. Click any blank area of the Stage or screen to de-select the oval.

8. This time, you'll use the Selection tool to select just a part of an object. As before, click and drag to begin creating a marquee around the oval—but this time, stop at roughly the halfway point, as shown in Figure 4.38. When you release the mouse button, the part of the oval that was overlapped by the marquee will be selected (see Figure 4.39); you can now move, recolor, resize, or reposition just this selected area. (You'll learn how to do all that in the next chapter.)

9. Click the Oval tool, press the J key on your keyboard, and create a new oval. (Pressing the J key activates the Object Drawing option, "welding" the outline and fill together.) Next, try to repeat step 8, but notice that you can't select only part of the object. That's because the Object Drawing option has been activated. To de-activate it, press the J key again.

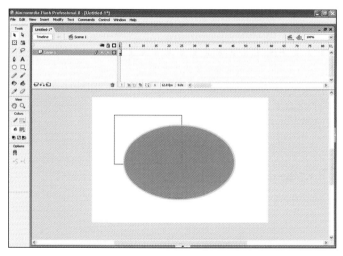

Figure 4.38 Create a marquee that only covers part of the oval.

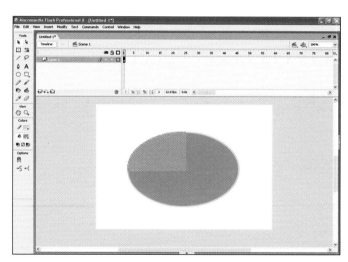

Figure 4.39 When you release the mouse button, only the part of the oval's fill and outline that is within the marquee will be selected.

4. Drawing, Selecting, and Importing Objects

Using the Lasso Tool

In step 8 of the previous section, you used the Selection tool to select part of an object. The Lasso tool takes things one step further, allowing you to select part of an object by drawing freehand over the desired area. This is particularly useful when you are selecting multiple objects or have objects that are close together. Here's how it works:

1. Start by creating a shape on the Stage, and then select the Lasso tool. (The Lasso tool is the third button down in the right column of the Tools panel.)

2. Click and drag to draw a freehand shape over the object. When you release the mouse button, a selection will be created in the shape of your freehand drawing. As with other selections, a mesh will appear, indicating the area that is selected (see Figure 4.40).

Using the Subselection Tool

When you use any of the selection tools I've mentioned so far, a mesh appears to indicate the selected area. When you select an object using the Subselection tool, however, the paths (that is, the lines and dots that define your shape) on the outline that make up the object will appear. This is particularly useful if you're reshaping an object. I'll talk a little more about reshaping objects later in this chapter; for now, just know that if you select an object's outline by drawing a marquee or clicking on it with the Subselection tool, a series of nodes (green squares) will appear around the object, as shown in Figure 4.41.

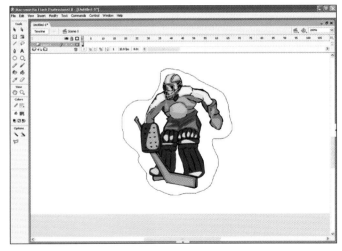

Figure 4.40 Using the Lasso tool, you can create a freehand selection that surrounds all or part of your object. Everything within the marquee that you draw will be selected when the mouse button is released.

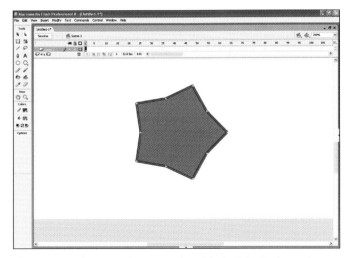

Figure 4.41 When you select an outline with the Subselection tool, green nodes appear around the outline.

Selecting Multiple Objects

A lot of the time, you'll want to apply changes to more than one object at once. It really doesn't matter which selection tool you use to do this; the process of selecting more than one object at once is the same. Here's what you do:

1. Draw five circles on the Stage, as shown in Figure 4.42.

2. One of the quickest ways to select multiple objects at once is to use the Selection tool to draw a marquee around them. To do so, click the Selection tool and position the mouse pointer above and to the left of the top-left circle. Then, click, drag the marquee around the three top circles, and release the mouse button. The three circles on the top level should now be selected, as shown in Figure 4.43.

3. Click any blank area of the Stage to deselect the circles.

4. Try using a marquee to select all the objects on the Stage except the circle in the middle on the top row. Impossible, isn't it? You can't create a marquee that surrounds all the circles without encompassing the middle circle. Try this: Create a marquee that surrounds all the objects. Then, hold down the Shift key and click and drag a marquee around the middle circle in the top row. This removes it from the selection, as shown in Figure 4.44.

5. As before, click any blank area to deselect the objects.

6. Rather than drawing a marquee, you can press the Shift key and click various object fills and outlines to select them. Click the fill of the circle in the middle of the top row; then, while pressing the Shift key, click the outlines and fills of other objects to select them, as shown in Figure 4.45. To deselect an object, click it while pressing the Shift key.

7. As before, click any blank area to deselect the objects.

8. You can also select multiple objects with the Lasso tool. Simply hold down the Shift key as you drag around the objects to select them.

9. As before, click any blank area to deselect the objects.

10. To quickly select all the objects on the Stage, press Ctrl+A.

11. As before, click any blank area to deselect the objects.

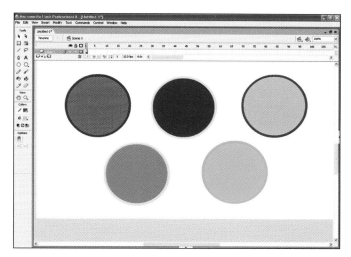

Figure 4.42 You can color the five circles, as shown here, but it isn't necessary. (You'll learn about coloring objects in the next chapter.)

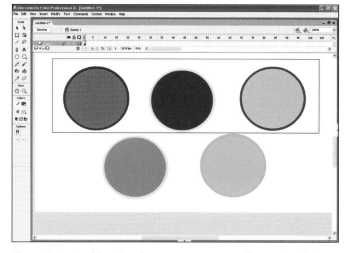

Figure 4.43 Anything that the marquee surrounds will be selected when the mouse button is released.

4. Drawing, Selecting, and Importing Objects

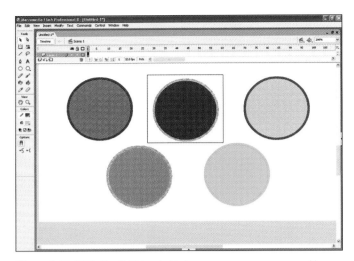

Figure 4.44 With the Shift key held down, you can remove—or add—areas to your selection.

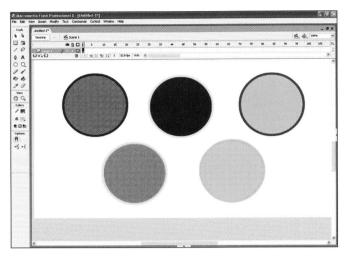

Figure 4.45 By holding down the Shift key and clicking different fills and outlines, you can add or remove them from your selection.

Importing Objects

Whether they're images from a clip-art CD, pictures you've downloaded from the web, or files friends have sent you, there are literally dozens of file types you can import into Flash. The actual process of importing is quite easy, involving only a few steps:

1. Open the File menu, choose Import, and select Import to Stage or click Ctrl+R to open the Import dialog box, shown in Figure 4.46.

2. Navigate to the folder on your computer that contains the file you want to import.

3. Double-click the file. The file will be imported onto the Stage, and can then be manipulated like any other object.

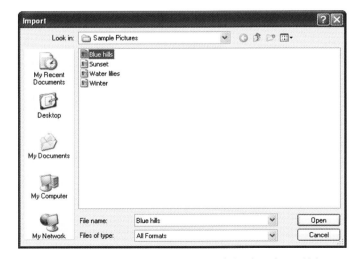

Figure 4.46 Press Ctrl+R to open the Import dialog box, from which you can select a file to download.

FILE TYPES

As mentioned, there are literally dozens of file types you can import into Flash. To see a complete list, click the Files of Type drop-down arrow in the Import dialog box, as shown in Figure 4.47. Even if you don't see the file type you are looking for, you still may be able to get the desired image into Flash using Copy and Paste commands. For example, I have a clip-art CD of images that are in CMX format, a CorelDRAW format. If I open the clip-art in CorelDRAW, I can copy it there and then paste it into Flash.

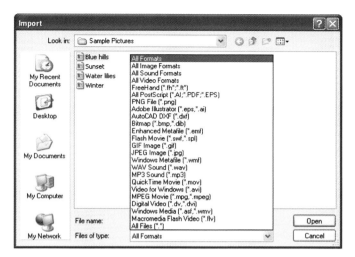

Figure 4.47 The Files of Type drop-down list shows you the various supported file formats.

4. Drawing, Selecting, and Importing Objects

chapter 5
Transforming and Filling Objects

O nce you have your objects created or imported and selected, there are a gazillion things you can do with them to get them to look just the way you want. I mean, when it comes to changing the objects you've created or imported, what *can't* Flash do? This chapter explores several dozen methods for adjusting the look of your objects. From coloring to rotating to skewing to squishing, I'll focus on the techniques you need to know to perfect your images. Understanding these techniques will not only help in the creation of your characters, objects, and backgrounds, but as you'll see in later chapters, they can be used to actually create your animations.

Moving Objects

Being able to move the objects that you have created is of vital importance when it comes to creating characters and animations. As you learned in Chapter 4, "Drawing, Selecting, and Importing Objects," in order to be able to move an object or series of objects, they must first be selected. (If you can't remember how to select objects, refer to Chapter 4.) Once an object is selected, it can be moved in one of several ways.

The easiest way to move an object is to simply drag it with the Selection tool. To do so, position the mouse pointer over the object, and click and drag it to the desired location. As you drag, a green outline of the object will appear, allowing you to preview the object's location; when you release the mouse button, the object will be moved to the same spot as the outline, as shown in Figure 5.1. This method also works if you opt for the Lasso tool or the Subselection tool to select your object; simply select the object, and then click within the selection and drag to move it. Another way to move an object is to select it, and then use the arrow keys on your keyboard to move it up, down, left, or right.

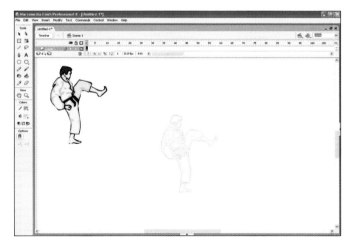

Figure 5.1 As you drag a selected object, a green outline will appear, enabling you to preview the object's new location.

SNAPPING

As you move an object across the Stage, you may notice that it doesn't seem to move freely, instead temporarily sticking to certain locations. This is due to the Snapping feature, which acts like a virtual magnet. This feature is useful if you want to precisely place the object at a location on the Stage, but can get annoying otherwise. You can turn snapping on or off by opening the View menu, choosing Snapping, and then clicking the snap option you want to enable or disable. (Those options with a checkmark beside them are already on.) Your options include the following:

◆ **Snap to Align.** This option is turned on by default. As you move one object close to another, a vertical or horizontal line will appear around the object you moved over, allowing you to align the object you are moving with other objects on the Stage.

◆ **Snap to Grid.** Have you ever used graph paper in a math or science class? If so, you know that using graph paper makes it way easier to line things up. That's exactly why the grid in Flash is so great—it creates non-printing vertical and horizontal lines on the Stage. Using this grid—which you display by opening the View menu, choosing Grid, and selecting Show Grid—you can quickly tell if objects are aligned. If you enable the Snap to Grid option, then the lines of the grid will act like magnets; as you move your object, it will temporarily stick to the grid lines.

◆ **Snap to Guides.** A *guide* is like a custom grid that you can create on your own. To create a guide, you must first turn on the rulers; to do so, open the View menu and choose Rulers. Then, position the mouse pointer over the horizontal or vertical ruler and click and drag to the Stage to create a guide, which you can use to align objects. When the Snap to Guides feature is enabled, if you move an object close to one of the guides you've created, the object will snap to it.

◆ **Snap to Pixels.** If you up the zoom to 400 percent or more, a pixel grid, which shows the pixel makeup of your animation, will appear. Turning on the Snap to Pixel feature will make the objects snap to the pixel grid.

◆ **Snap to Objects.** Enabling this feature will turn all the objects on the Stage into magnets. As you move one object close to another, the two objects will snap together.

ALIGNING OBJECTS

Although the snapping feature can be used to help you align your objects, Flash actually has a tool that's specifically designed to help you align and distribute (space out) your objects. You can align your objects along their edges either horizontally or vertically. Here's how:

1. Select the objects you would like to align or distribute, as shown in Figure 5.2.

2. Open the Modify menu, choose Align, and then select one of the many alignment and distribution options, as shown in Figure 5.3. The selected objects will be aligned or distributed based on your selection.

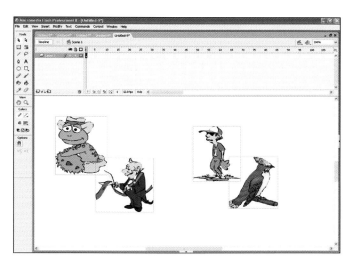

Figure 5.2 Select the objects you want to align using any one of the selection methods.

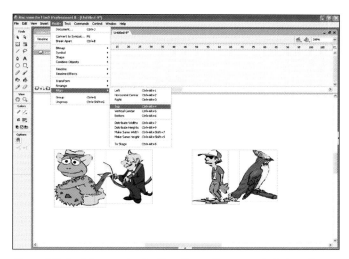

Figure 5.3 In this example, the Top align option was selected, so the images are aligned horizontally across the top.

Free Transforming—a.k.a. Moving, Resizing, Squishing, Stretching, Skewing, and Rotating

The Free Transform tool is the Swiss Army knife of Flash—it can do so many different things! Whether you want to move an object, resize it, rotate it, squish it, or stretch it, the Free Transform tool is the tool for you. Although you can accomplish most of these tasks with other tools and the Property inspector, the Free Transform tool, located just under the Selection tool in the Tools panel, is very easy to access and use. Simply click the tool, click on the object that you would like to manipulate (see Figure 5.4), and you'll be ready to transform it.

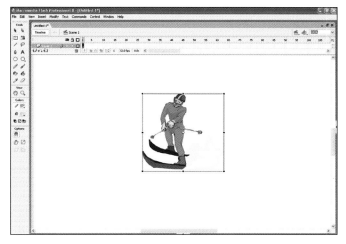

Figure 5.4 When you select an object with the Free Transform tool, a box with a series of handles (black boxes) will appear around your object.

5. Transforming and Filling Objects

61

Moving an Object

Moving an object with the Free Transform tool is very similar to moving an object with any of the other selection tools. After clicking the Free Transform tool, simply position the mouse pointer over the object you'd like to move (the mouse pointer will turn into a pointer with a four-sided arrow, as shown in Figure 5.5), click, and drag the object to a new location. As you drag, a preview of the new location will appear.

Resizing an Object

Resizing an object with the Free Transform tool is simply a matter of positioning the mouse pointer in the right place—the "right place" being over any of the corner handles. When your mouse pointer is over any of the corner handles, it will turn into a double-sided arrow; just click and drag inward to reduce the size of an object or outward to make it larger. As you drag, a preview of the new size of the shape will appear, as shown in Figure 5.6.

Squishing and Stretching an Object

Ever wish you could gain or lose weight instantly? Using the Free Transform tool, your objects can. By simply clicking and dragging over any of the object's side handles, you can squish or stretch an object. Dragging inward squishes your objects, and dragging outward stretches them. Just as with moving and resizing, a green outline will appear showing you a preview of the new shape of the object (see Figure 5.7).

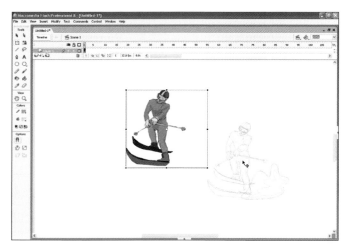

Figure 5.5 Notice how the mouse pointer changes when it is over the object.

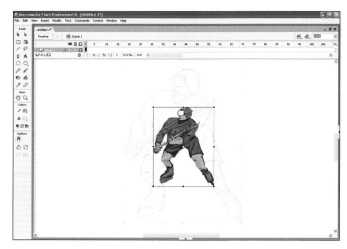

Figure 5.6 As you drag any of the corner handles, the image is resized. A green preview of the image will show the new object size.

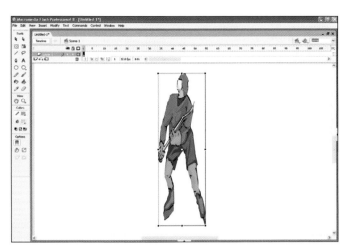

Figure 5.7 By clicking any of the side handles and dragging inward or outward, you can squish or stretch your object.

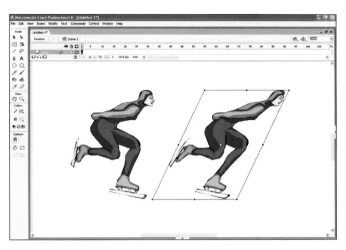

Figure 5.8 The image on the right has been skewed.

Skewing an Object

If you're not sure what "skewing" means, visualize the letter I when it has been italicized. Notice how it looks like it has been pushed over, like so: *I*. That's exactly what skewing does. It makes an object look like it has been tilted. You can tilt it up or down, or to one side or the other.

To skew an object, place the mouse pointer anywhere between the handles on the black line that surrounds the object. You'll know you are in the right spot when the mouse pointer changes into two half arrows pointing in different directions. Then, click and drag the line in the direction you want the object to be skewed, as shown in Figure 5.8.

Rotating an Object

To rotate an object with the Free Transform tool, you need to position the mouse pointer just outside any one of the corner handles. The mouse pointer will turn into a circle with an arrow to indicate that you are in the right place. Once the mouse pointer has changed, you can click and drag the mouse pointer in a circular motion, clockwise or counterclockwise, to rotate the object (see Figure 5.9).

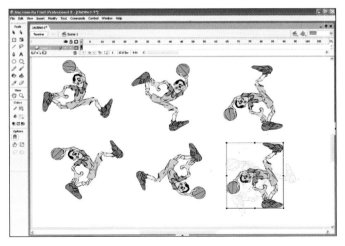

Figure 5.9 The original image is in the top-left corner; the others have been rotated in varying degrees in different directions.

By default, the center of rotation—that is, the point around which the object is rotated—is in the middle of the object. Think of a wheel on a bicycle: It spins around and around the hub at the wheel's center; the hub, then, is the center of rotation. But what if you want the center of rotation for your object to be located elsewhere? In Flash, the center of rotation can be moved to any location. Here's how you do it:

1. Click the object you want to rotate with the Free Transform tool. The object will be surrounded by handles, and you'll notice a white dot in the middle of the object. That white dot indicates the center of rotation.

2. Click and drag the white dot to a new location, as shown in Figure 5.10.

3. Position the mouse pointer just outside any of the corner handles. When the mouse pointer turns into a partial circle, you are ready to rotate; click and drag in a circular motion, and the object will rotate around the new center of rotation, as shown in Figure 5.11.

FREE-TRANSFORMING TEXT

Moving, resizing, squishing, stretching, skewing, and rotating text is a little different from other objects. Although text *can* be resized, stretched, skewed, and so on with the Free Transform tool, you *can't* change the shape of text without first breaking it apart. To break text apart, do the following:

1. Right-click the first letter of the text and choose Break Apart from the menu that appears.

2. Repeat this step on each individual letter within the text block.

3. After the text is completely broken apart, you can reshape it with the Free Transform tool as normal. To do this, click a blank area to deselect the text and then click on the individual letter that you would like to reshape.

Figure 5.10 Position the white dot, the center of rotation, at a new location by clicking and dragging.

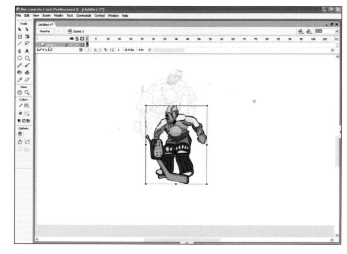

Figure 5.11 Notice how the object rotates around the new center of rotation.

Reshaping an Object

Let's face it: Unless you are making animations for kindergarteners—and maybe not even then—basic circles, squares, and stars just won't do when it comes to creating shapes. The good news is that you can use those basic shapes to create many types of more complex shapes by manipulating them. There are actually several ways you can reshape and change the properties of your objects, using a variety of methods—selections, the Property inspector, and more.

Reshaping with Selections

If you're like me, you may not be the best artist in the world. That's okay! With Flash, you don't have to be. You can create some wild, wonderful, and wacky shapes through the use of selections. Using either the Selection tool or the Lasso tool, you can select part of an object and then delete that selection to create some interesting shapes. Have you ever seen a pie chart with a section of the pie removed? That's exactly what you'll create here:

1. Start by creating a large circle in the middle of the Stage.

2. Next, create a selection that overlaps the top-left corner of the circle, as shown in Figure 5.12.

3. Position the mouse pointer over the selection, and then click and drag upward and slightly to the left to move the selected piece away from the circle, as shown in Figure 5.13.

4. You can either delete the selection, leaving you with only one shape, or opt to keep them both. To delete the selection—or any selected object, for that matter—simply press the Delete key on your keyboard.

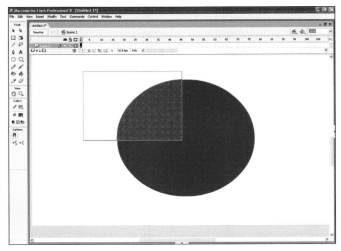

Figure 5.12 Use the Selection tool to select an area in the top-left corner of the circle.

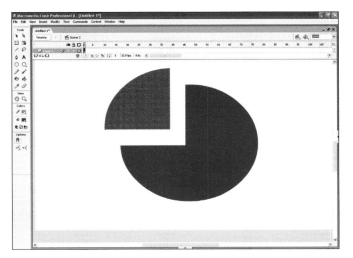

Figure 5.13 By moving the selection, you create two interesting-looking shapes.

CUTTING, COPYING, DUPLICATING, AND PASTING OBJECTS

Once you have an object selected, you can copy it (Ctrl+C), cut it (Ctrl+X), duplicate it (Ctrl+D), or paste it (Ctrl+V) using keyboard shortcuts. Copying and cutting places the selected object on the clipboard; duplicating the selected object means you make a copy of it without putting it on the system clipboard first.

Reshaping Objects with Other Shapes

Another way to create interesting objects on your Stage is to use other shapes. Have you ever made cookies with a cookie cutter? You can apply the same principle to your shapes with Flash, using one shape as a "cookie cutter" to cut away from another. Here's how this works:

> Before you begin, make sure the Object Drawing button in the Options section of the Tools panel is not selected.

1. Create two circles, as shown in Figure 5.14. (The two circles don't necessarily have to be the same colors as the ones shown here.)

2. Using whatever method you prefer, select the circle on the right and then move it so that it overlaps the circle on the left (see Figure 5.15).

3. Click any blank area of the Stage to deselect the circle.

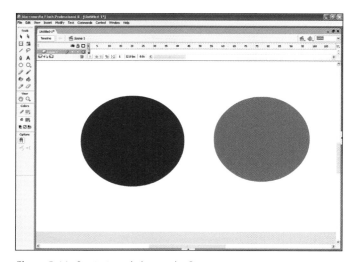

Figure 5.14 Create two circles on the Stage.

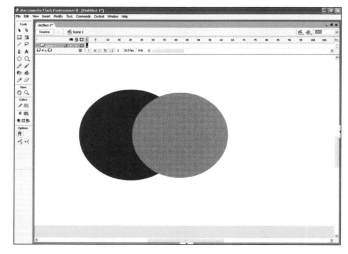

Figure 5.15 Move the circle on the right so that it overlaps the circle on the left.

4. Click the same circle again to select it. Then, while pressing the Shift key, click the outline of the circle to select both the outline and the fill.

5. Press the Delete key; you'll be left with the partial moon shown in Figure 5.16.

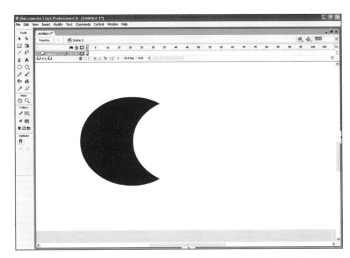

OVERLAPPING SHAPES

Oh no! What happens if you overlap one shape on another—but didn't mean to? Unfortunately, the bottom shape will, in essence, be gone because it can no longer be completely selected. To see what I mean, create a circle, and then create a square that partially overlaps the circle. Try to select the entire circle now—you can't. You can only select the part of the circle peeking out from behind the square. This could pose a problem if you want to use the full circle again. To avoid this problem, press the J key on your keyboard to activate the Object Drawing feature. This will group together the fill and the outline; when selected, the object will stay as one, even if there is another object over the top of it.

Figure 5.16 You can create interesting shapes by using other shapes as "cookie cutters."

CHANGING OBJECT ORDER

The order in which objects appear on the Stage depends on the order in which they are created. For example, say you create an oval and then create a rectangle. If you move the rectangle object over the oval, the rectangle will be on *top* of the oval. If you want the oval to be on top of the rectangle, you'll need to change its order.

1. Click the Oval tool.

2. Click the Object Drawing button or press the letter J to ensure that Object Drawing mode is enabled. That way, you'll be able to select both shapes individually, even when they overlap.

3. Create an oval anywhere on the Stage.

4. Click the Rectangle tool and create a rectangle on the Stage.

5. Move the rectangle so that it overlaps the oval. Because the rectangle was created last, it will appear on top of the oval, as shown in Figure 5.17.

6. With the rectangle selected (it will be selected right after you create it), open the Modify menu and choose Arrange to see your arrangement options. They are as follows:

◆ **Bring to Front.** This brings the selected object to the front all objects.

◆ **Bring Forward.** This brings the selected object forward by one level.

◆ **Send Backwards.** This places the selected object behind all others.

◆ **Send to Back.** This sends the selected object back one level.

◆ **Lock.** This locks the selected object so that it can't be selected or moved.

◆ **Unlock All.** This unlocks all your locked objects.

7. Click the Send to Back option to place the rectangle behind all other objects on the Stage, as shown in Figure 5.18.

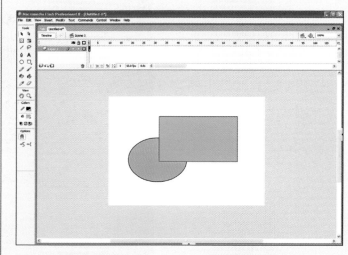

Figure 5.17 Because the rectangle was created last, it appears on top of the oval.

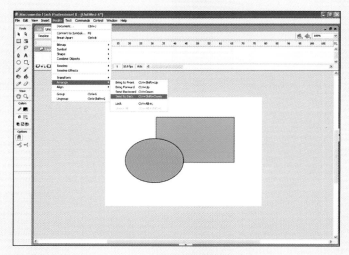

Figure 5.18 When you select the Send to Back option, the rectangle is placed behind the oval.

You can also create interesting shapes by combining two objects together. Give this a try:

1. Create two overlapping ovals with the same color fill and outline, as shown in Figure 5.19.

2. You can also combine two or more objects that *don't* have the same outline color. To begin, create two ovals that overlap, but whose outlines are a different color than their fills, as shown in Figure 5.20.

3. With the Selection tool, click the part of the outline that overlaps the ovals to select it and it alone.

4. Press the Delete key on your keyboard; you'll be left with the shape you see in Figure 5.21.

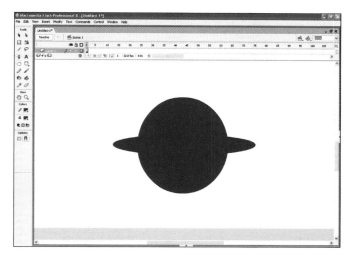

Figure 5.19 When two shapes of the same color and outline overlap, they become as one.

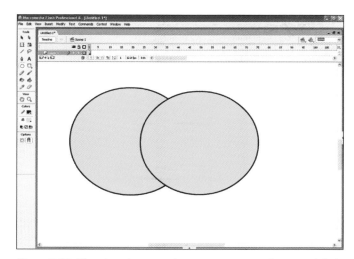

Figure 5.20 When two shapes overlap, you can remove the parts of their outlines that overlap to make one shape.

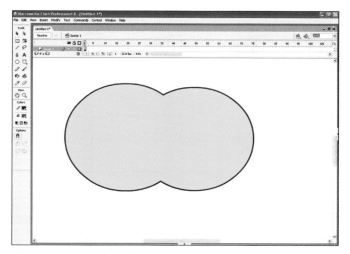

Figure 5.21 When the outline that overlaps the two shapes is deleted, you are left with an interesting-looking shape.

Reshaping with the Subselection Tool

The Subselection tool lets you to change the shape and outline of your object. Your outlines consist of little marks called *anchor points* that make up the shape. The outline of an object becomes like Silly Putty when it is selected with the Subselection tool; that is, you can move the anchor points around to reshape the line segments.

Moving Anchor Points

When you move an object's anchor points with the Subselection tool, the fill of the object will move along with it. Here's how it's done:

1. Create any type of shape.

2. Select the outline of the shape with the Subselection tool. A series of green anchor points will appear around the outline, as shown in Figure 5.22.

3. Position your mouse pointer over any of the anchor points, click, and drag inward or outward. The outline reshaped as you drag. When you release the mouse button, you'll see that not only has the outline changed shape, but the fill within the outline has changed to accommodate the new shape (see Figure 5.23).

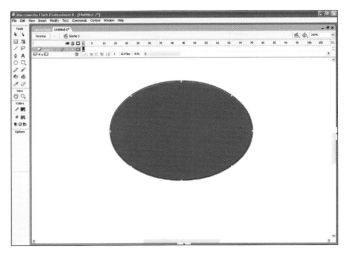

Figure 5.22 When you click an object's outline with the Subselection tool, the anchor points that make up the line appear in green.

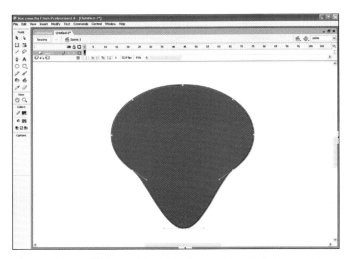

Figure 5.23 By clicking and dragging downward on the bottom anchor point of this oval, I was able to create this interesting shape. Looks like an alien, doesn't it?

Curving Segments

You may have noticed in the last section that when you clicked an anchor point, a short green line attached itself to that anchor point. This line is called a *tangent* and can be used to curve the outline. Here's how:

1. Create any type of shape.

2. Select the outline with the Subselection tool.

3. Click any of the anchor points. A tangent will appear not only on the anchor point you clicked, but also on the two anchor points on either side of the one you selected, as shown in Figure 5.24.

4. Notice the two little green circles at each end of tangent attached to the anchor point. Click and drag any of these circles up or down to curve the line segment. You can repeat this for any other segments, as shown in Figure 5.25.

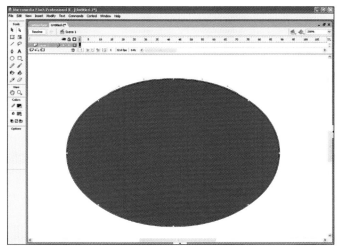

Figure 5.24 A tangent appears across the anchor point that you click.

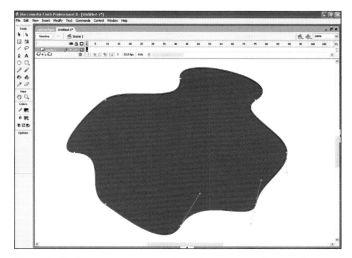

Figure 5.25 You can curve any anchor point to create all sorts of wonderful shapes.

Resizing and Reshaping with the Property Inspector

In the last chapter, you briefly explored using the Property inspector to change the size, style, and color of an outline and a fill. In addition to changing those properties, you can use the Property inspector to change the size and position of your shape. If the Property inspector is not already open, press Ctrl+F5 to launch it at the bottom of the screen.

Once you have selected an object, depending on how the shape was created or where it was imported from, there will be a variety of properties you can change in the Property inspector. In the bottom-left corner of the Property inspector, you'll notice that there are four boxes labeled W, H, X, and Y. The W and H boxes represent the width and height in pixels of the objects in your selection (see Figure 5.26).

Figure 5.26 These four boxes allow you to adjust the size and location of the object you have selected.

You can change these numbers to increase or decrease the size of the objects in your selection. You can even squish or stretch your selection by entering a set of disproportionate numbers in these boxes. Confused? Say you have selected a circle whose width and height are both 100 pixels. If you changed the height of the circle to 200 pixels, then the object would be stretched out (see Figure 5.27). In other words, using the Property inspector, you can not only change the size of a selected object, you can also squish and stretch it.

You may have noticed a little lock icon just to the left of the W and H boxes. By clicking this icon, you can unlock or lock the proportion setting. If the setting is locked, the ratio of width to height will always stay the same for your selection. For example, say you have selected a square that is 100×200. If the proportion setting is locked and you change the width to 50, the height would automatically change to 100 to stay in proportion to the original selection.

The X and Y boxes specify where on the Stage your selected object is located. In other words, you can use these two boxes to move your selections around the screen. The X number indicates the selection's horizontal position (left and right) and the Y number indicates the vertical position (up and down).

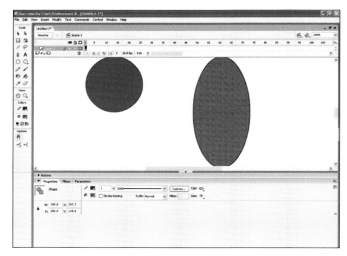

Figure 5.27 The circle on the left is 100×100 pixels. The oval on the right has been stretched to 100×200 using the Property inspector.

Applying Fills and Outlines

No animation is complete without color—that is, of course, if you're not making a black-and-white animation! Color can make or break your animations. It can help your objects stand out, convey messages and emotion, and draw attention to certain areas. Because of color's importance, Flash provides you with a variety of ways in which you can color your fills and outlines; the method you end up using will depend on your personal preference and the type of project you are creating. Solid colors are only one option for fills and outlines. Flash also provides you with tools to create different *gradient fills*, which are fills that consist of two or more colors. In this section, you'll look at different ways to both select and apply colors to your objects.

Selecting Colors

Flash gives you a bunch of options for selecting the colors you want to apply to your fills and outlines. Once you have a color selected, that color is "loaded," and will be the default color until it is changed.

> It's best to specify a color for an object's fill and outline before you create it. That being said, an object's color can be changed after the object has been created. Simply select the object using one of the selection methods and then load a different color.

Using the Tools Panel

Perhaps the easiest way to specify a color for an object's fill and its stroke (that is, its outline) to select a color from the Colors section of the Tools panel. Notice that the Tools panel features two color buttons; the top one specifies the stroke color, and the bottom one specifies the fill color. When you click either button, you will be presented with a palette of colors from which to choose, as shown in Figure 5.28. Simply click a color to load it.

If those swatches don't provide enough color options for you, you can open the Color dialog box. This dialog box lets you to create just about any color in the rainbow. Here's how it's done:

1. Click either the Fill Color or Outline Color button on the Tools panel. A series of swatches appears.

2. Click the button that shows a color wheel, found in the top-right corner of the swatches (see Figure 5.29). This opens the Color dialog box.

3. On the right side of the dialog box, you'll see a square with many different shades of color. Click the desired hue within that box; when you do, a cross-hair will appear where you clicked, and a swatch of the selected color will be displayed near the bottom of the dialog box (see Figure 5.30).

Figure 5.28 When the Color Fill button is clicked, a palette of colors appears.

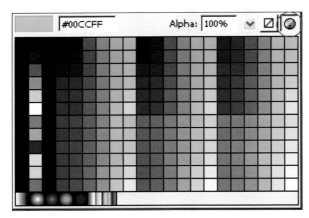

Figure 5.29 Click the button in the top-right corner of the swatches to open the Color dialog box.

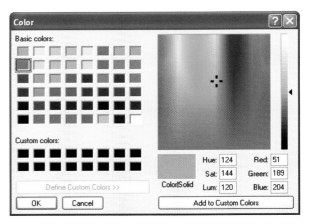

Figure 5.30 The Color dialog box allows you to create just about any color.

4. On the far right side of the dialog box, you'll see a thin strip of color with a black triangle beside it. Click and drag the black triangle up or down to adjust the brightness of the color you selected. Once again, a swatch of the color will appear at the bottom of the dialog box.

5. Once you have the color the way you like it, click OK to load that color.

COLOR MIXER

By pressing Shift+F9, you can open a palette on the side of your screen called the Color Mixer, which works in much the same way as the Color dialog box. The advantage of the Color Mixer is that it can be kept open on the side of your screen to give you quick access to colors.

Using the Eyedropper Tool

Another clever tool for choosing colors is the Eyedropper tool. It enables you to select a color from any object on your Stage. This tool is particularly useful if you have imported a photograph onto your Stage—you can use it to select any color in your photograph to use as the fill. Once you use the Eyedropper tool to select a color, it automatically changes to the Paint Bucket tool or the Ink Bottle tool so that you can apply the color to an object, depending on where you click. Here's how it works:

1. Create two shapes on the Stage, each with a different outline and fill color, as shown in Figure 5.31. (I drew ovals, but you could use anything, even a photograph.)

2. Click the Eyedropper tool.

Flash Animation for Teens

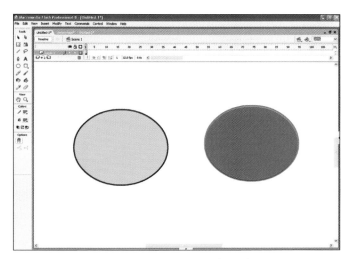

Figure 5.31 Create two shapes, each with different fill and outline colors.

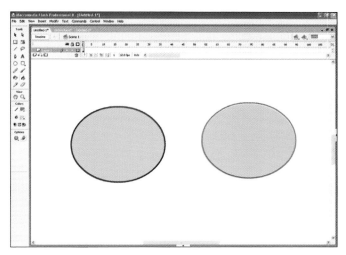

Figure 5.32 The Eyedropper tool turns into the Paint Bucket tool as soon as you pick a color.

3. Click once in the middle of the oval on the left. The mouse pointer will change from the Eyedropper tool to the Paint Bucket tool, with the color you selected loaded.

4. Click the oval on the right, and the fill color will be applied (see Figure 5.32).

5. Click the Eyedropper tool again, but this time click the outline of the oval on the right. The outline color will be loaded, but this time the Eyedropper tool will change to the Ink Bottle tool, which is used to apply an outline color to an object.

6. Click on the oval on the left (you can click anywhere on the oval, not just the outline) and the loaded color will be applied (see Figure 5.33).

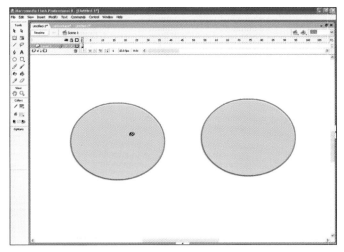

Figure 5.33 The Eyedropper tool changes to the Ink Bottle tool when an outline color is selected.

Other Color Options

At the bottom of the of the Colors section of the Tools panel, you'll find three buttons, each of which can be used to set colors:

◆ **Black and white.** Select this option to color the outline black and the fill white.

◆ **No color.** Click this to remove the color from the selected object.

◆ **Swap colors.** Select this to make the fill color the outline color and vice versa.

Applying Colors

In the last section, you learned not only how to select colors with the Eyedropper tool, but also how to apply those colors because the Eyedropper tool automatically switches to either the Paint Bucket or Ink Bottle tools. This section explores those tools a little more, along with the many other methods for applying colors to your objects.

Using the Colors Section of the Tools Panel

Perhaps the easiest way to apply a color to a shape is to first select the shape using any of the selection tools, and then to select the desired colors using the Fill Color and Stroke Color buttons in the Tools panel.

Using the Paint Bucket Tool to Apply Fill Colors

If you'd rather not have to select an object before applying a color to it, you can use the Paint Bucket tool. The Paint Bucket tool applies the selected fill color to any object that you click. Let's go through an example.

1. Create several different-colored shapes on the Stage, as shown in Figure 5.34.

2. Select a fill color using any one of the color-selection methods outlined earlier, and then click the Paint Bucket tool. (Alternatively, press the K key on your keyboard to select this tool.)

3. Click all of the shapes. As you click them, the fill color will be applied, as shown in Figure 5.35.

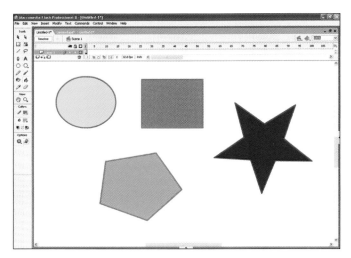

Figure 5.34 Create several different-colored shapes on the screen.

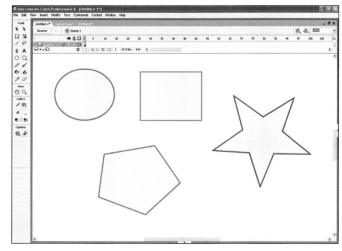

Figure 5.35 When you click on objects with the Paint Bucket tool, the selected fill color is applied.

Using the Ink Bottle Tool to Apply Outline/Stroke Colors

The Ink Bottle tool works in the exact same way as the Paint Bucket tool, except that the Ink Bottle tool applies outline/stroke colors and the Paint Bucket tool applies fill colors. Once you have an outline color selected, simply click any object (you can click on the object itself; you don't need to click on the outline) and the outline color will be applied (see Figure 5.36).

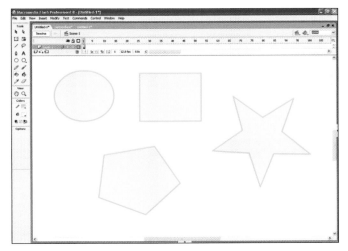

Figure 5.36 The Ink Bottle tool allows you to quickly change the stroke color of an object.

APPLYING COLOR WITH THE PROPERTY INSPECTOR

You can use the Property inspector to change the color of the outline, fill, and other properties of your object. Depending on what type of object(s) you have in your selection, different options will be available. If you click the Fill Color or Stroke Color button, a palette of color swatches from which you can choose will appear, as illustrated in Figure 5.37. As soon as you select a color, that change will be reflected in your selection. You typically can also use the Property inspector to change the style and thickness of the selected object's outline.

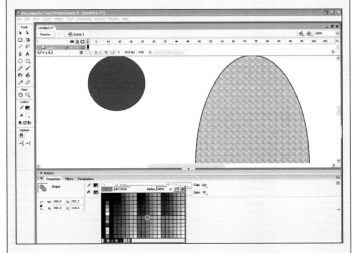

Figure 5.37 Fill color is one of the many things you can change with the Property inspector.

Now You Try

Let's pause for a moment and put to use some of the things you've learned so far in the book. To begin, try to re-create the cartoon character you see in Figure 5.38.

If you can't quite get it, don't worry. Just follow these steps:

1. Start by creating three ovals with a yellow fill and black outline, positioning them as shown in Figure 5.39.

2. Using the Selection tool, click on the portion of the outline that separates one of the smaller ovals from the larger one and press the Delete key on your keyboard to remove this part of the outline (see Figure 5.40). Repeat this step for the other ear.

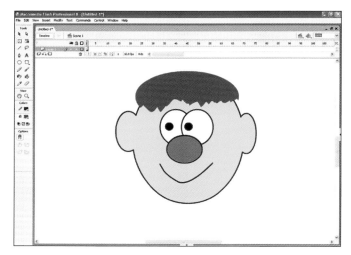

Figure 5.38 Try to re-create the cartoon face you see here.

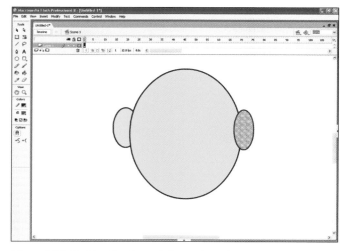

Figure 5.39 Position the three circles as shown here.

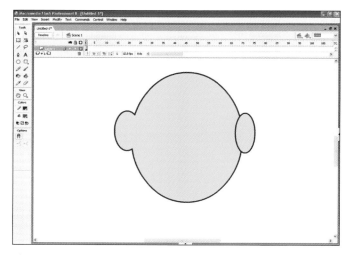

Figure 5.40 Remove the part of the outline where the ovals overlap.

78

3. Create two white ovals with black outlines that slightly overlap, as you see in Figure 5.41.

4. Create two black circles and place them on the two ovals. These will act as the pupils.

5. Select the two eyeballs using whichever selection method you prefer, click the selection, and drag it onto the face as shown in Figure 5.42.

6. Now it's time for the nose. Create a red circle and place it right under the eyes as shown in Figure 5.43.

7. To create the mouth, you'll use the Pen tool, just as you did in the last chapter. Click once in any blank area of the page, move the mouse pointer about a half inch to the right, and then click and drag upward and to the right until the line looks like a smile.

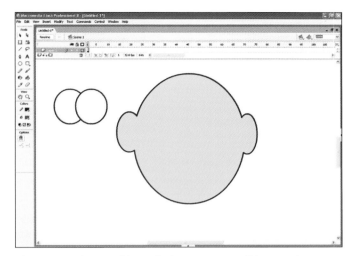

Figure 5.41 The two white ovals that you create will become the eyeballs.

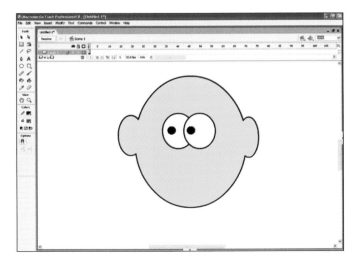

Figure 5.42 Place the two eyeballs on the face as shown here.

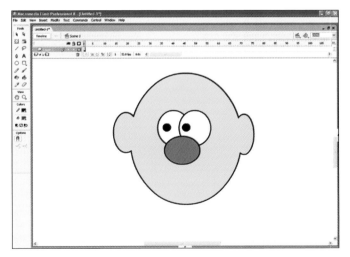

Figure 5.43 Place the nose right under the eyes, as shown here.

5. Transforming and Filling Objects

8. Select the smile and drag it onto the face, as shown in Figure 5.44.

9. To create the hair for this character, start by drawing an oval that is approximately as wide as the character's head. Then, remove part of the oval by using the Lasso tool to draw a rough freehand selection along the bottom half of the oval, as shown in Figure 5.45.

10. Press the Delete key on the keyboard to remove the bottom part of the oval. You'll be left with a shape like the one shown in Figure 5.46.

11. To remove the partial outline around the hair, select it using the Selection tool and then press the Delete key.

12. Select the hair and position it on the head, as shown in Figure 5.47.

13. Odds are the hair didn't fit perfectly on your character's head. To make it appear a bit more natural, click the Free Transform tool and drag the far-right middle handle to the right to stretch out the hair horizontally.

14. Next, position the mouse pointer over the bottom-middle handle, click, and drag downward to stretch the hair vertically, as shown in Figure 5.48. That's it!

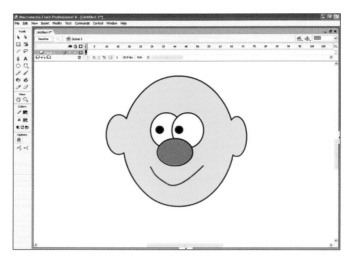

Figure 5.44 Create a smile with the Pen tool and then position it on the face.

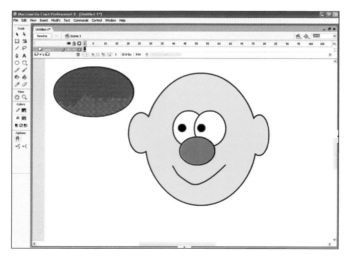

Figure 5.45 Create a rough selection along the bottom half of the oval, as shown here.

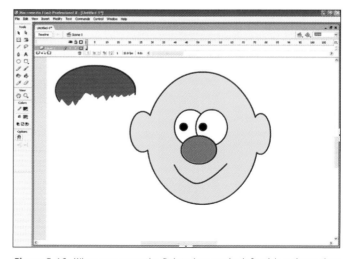

Figure 5.46 When you press the Delete key, you're left with a shape that you will use as the hair.

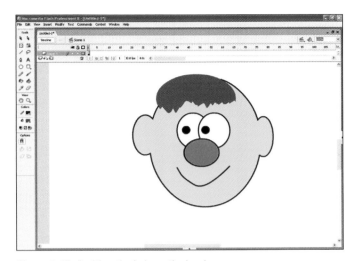

Figure 5.47 Position the hair on the head.

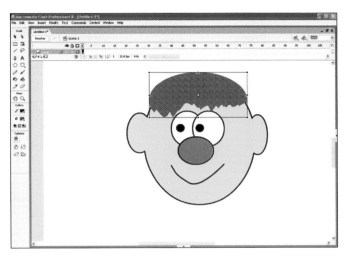

Figure 5.48 By clicking and dragging on the handles, you can stretch the hair out to fit the head as shown here.

GROUPING OBJECTS

The face you just created is made up of a variety of objects. If you want to move the face around, you have to select all the objects that make up the face before you can move it—which can be a pain if there are a lot of objects involved. An easier way is to group the objects in the face. Once objects are grouped, you can just select and move the group rather than selecting each component separately. In addition to making it easier to move things, grouping objects together ensures that the grouped object won't be affected by other objects that are moved on top of it. Remember when I mentioned the danger of inadvertently moving one object on top of another? That is, when one object is moved on top of another, the object on the bottom will in essence be lost because it can no longer be selected. This can be prevented if you first group the bottom object.

1. Using any one of the selection methods, select all the objects that you want included in the group.

2. Press Ctrl+G on the keyboard; the selected items will be grouped together, and will act as one object.

Even after you group objects together, you can still edit the parts that make up the group. Simply double-click the grouped object with the Selection tool. Notice that all other objects on the page are dimmed; you can now edit the objects, changing their colors or manipulating them in some other way. When you are finished, double-click on any blank area of the Stage; the dimmed objects will now reappear. If you decide you no longer want the objects to be grouped, simply select the group, open the Modify menu, and choose Ungroup.

SAVING YOUR CHARACTERS FOR RE-USE

Imagine that you've created a main character for your animation—like the cartoon character you just made. You're probably going to need to use that character over and over. Rather than having to re-create the character whenever you need it, Flash allows you to store your character as a symbol so that you can use it over and over. You can create a whole library of different symbols for repeated use in your animations.

1. Select the object that you want to re-use.

2. Press F8 to open the Convert to Symbol dialog box.

3. Type a name for your object in the dialog box and ensure that the Graphic option button is selected, as shown in Figure 5.49.

4. Click OK. Your symbol will be saved to the library.

5. Press Ctrl+L to open the library if it is not already open.

6. In the library, you'll notice all the shapes that you've added to it. You can click and drag any one of these symbols from the library to the Stage, as shown in Figure 5.50.

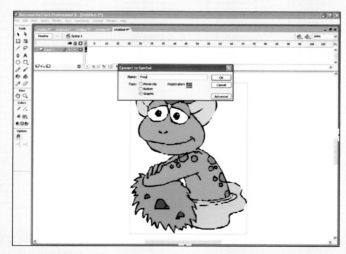

Figure 5.49 In the Convert to Symbol dialog box, you can name and categorize your symbol.

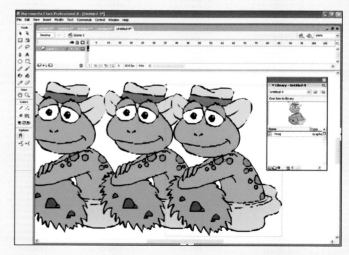

Figure 5.50 You can click and drag symbols from the library onto the Stage.

Using Gradient Fills

In addition to allowing you to apply solid-color fills to your objects, Flash lets you to create multi-colored fills called *gradients*. Gradients can help make your objects look more realistic because they create the illusion of lighting. There are two different types of gradient fills: radial fills, which are applied in a circular pattern, and linear fills, which are applied in a straight line. In addition to selecting the type of gradient fill, you can also change the number of colors in the gradient fill and its direction.

Applying a Gradient Fill

Applying gradients works in much the same way as applying solid-color fills. You simply choose one of several pre-set gradient fills

1. Click the Fill Color button. At the bottom of the palette of swatches that appears, you'll see some pre-set gradient options, as shown in Figure 5.51. Click any one of these options.

2. Select a shape tool—say, the Oval tool—and then click and drag on the Stage to create that shape. The gradient you selected will be the fill of the shape, as shown in Figure 5.52.

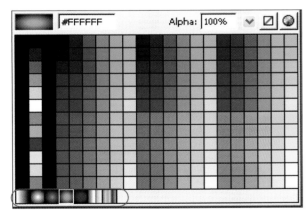

Figure 5.51 Select from any of the gradient options under the swatches.

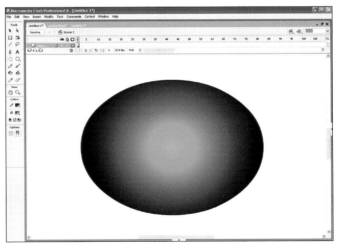

Figure 5.52 The gradient you selected as the fill appears in the shape.

5. Transforming and Filling Objects

Changing Gradient Types

There are pre-sets of both types of gradient fills—radial and linear—in the swatch palette that appears when you click the Fill Color button. If you select the wrong type of gradient fill by accident, you can use the Color Mixer (press Shift+F9 to open it) to change the gradient type, as shown in Figure 5.53. (This figure also illustrates the difference between a linear gradient fill and a radial fill.) Alternatively, you can simply select the object and choose a new gradient fill from the Fill Color palette.

> Gradient fills are not just for the fills of objects; they can also be applied to strokes. Just select the stroke (that is, the outline) before applying the gradient.

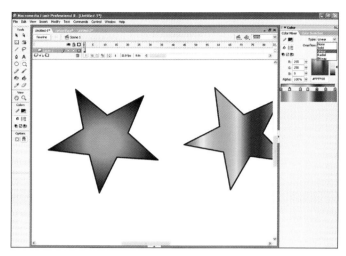

Figure 5.53 The star on the left has a radial gradient and the one on the right has a linear gradient. The Color Mixer allows you to change the type of gradient.

Changing the Gradient Colors

Flash gives you just a few pre-sets for gradient colors, but that's okay because you can create your own gradient colors using the Color Mixer.

1. Start by selecting a shape that already has a gradient fill.

2. If the Color Mixer isn't already open, press Shift+F9 to open it.

3. Notice the thin horizontal bar of color in the Color Mixer; underneath it are small swatches for each color in the gradient. Drag any one of those color swatches left or right to reposition it; notice how the colors in your shape move as you drag the color swatch (see Figure 5.54).

4. To add a color to the gradient, position the mouse pointer in a blank area under the thin color line in the Color Mixer (you'll know you are in the right place because a plus sign will appear next to the mouse pointer). Click once; a color will be added at that location (see Figure 5.55).

5. To change one of the colors within the gradient, click the swatch for the gradient color you'd like to change and then click any color in the large square of colors beside the RGB fields in the Color Mixer or enter the color's red, green, and blue values in the R, G, and B fields, respectively. The color in the gradient will be changed to the color you selected.

Modifying Gradients with the Gradient Transform Tool

So far you've learned how to select, apply, and change the color of your gradient fills. If you're interested in changing the position of a gradient fill, rotating it, squishing it, or stretching it, you use the Gradient Transform tool.

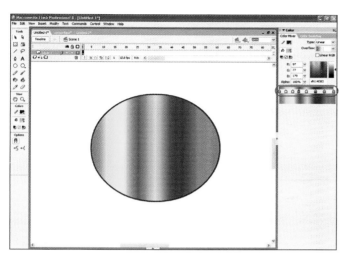

Figure 5.54 As you move a swatch in the Color Mixer, the color moves within the shape.

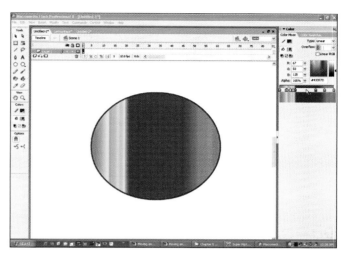

Figure 5.55 Click in the blank area under the thin color line to add a color to the gradient.

1. Select the Gradient Transform tool.

2. Click any shape with a gradient fill. You'll notice a few changes to your shape. First, there will be two blue lines surrounding the gradient, with a square attached to one of the lines. At the top of one of the lines, you'll notice a circle with a small arrow attached to it. Finally, in the middle of the gradient, you'll notice a white circle.

3. Position the mouse pointer over the small square, click, and drag inward or outward to squish or stretch the fill, as shown in Figure 5.56.

4. Position the mouse pointer over the white circle in the middle of the gradient, click, and drag the circle to change the center point of your fill, as shown in Figure 5.57.

5. Position the mouse pointer over the circle at the top of one of the blue lines, click, and drag to can rotate the gradient (see Figure 5.58).

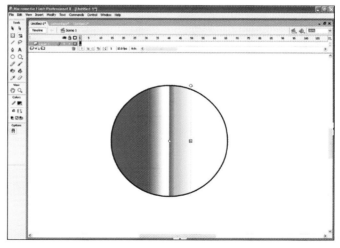

Figure 5.56 As you drag inward or outward, you squish or stretch the fill.

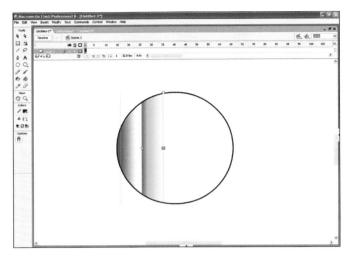

Figure 5.57 By clicking and dragging the white circle within the gradient fill, you can reposition the gradient's center point.

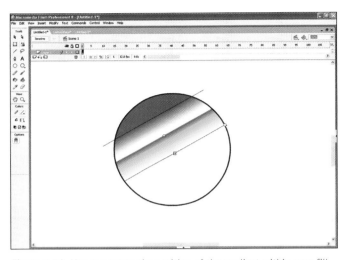

Figure 5.58 You can rotate the position of the gradient within your fill.

Now You Try

Attempt to re-create the fill of the circle shown in Figure 5.59. To get you started, the circle has a white and red radial fill, with the center point positioned in the top-left corner.

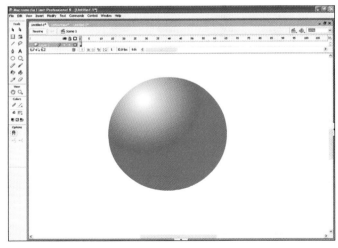

Figure 5.59 Try to re-create this 3D sphere by applying a radial fill.

If you can't quite get it on your own, follow these steps:

1. In the Colors section of the Tools panel, select No Outline for the outline color, and then choose the black and red radial pre-set for the fill (see Figure 5.60).

2. Select the Oval tool from the Tools panel.

3. While holding down the Shift key, click and drag to create a circle on the Stage; when you release the mouse button, the circle should have a red and black radial fill, as shown in Figure 5.61.

4. Choose the Selection tool and select the circle.

5. Press Shift+F9 to open the Color Mixer, which you'll use to change the black color to white and the white color to red.

6. Click the red color swatch in the Color Mixer to select it.

7. Type 255 in the R, G, and B boxes.

8. Click on the black swatch.

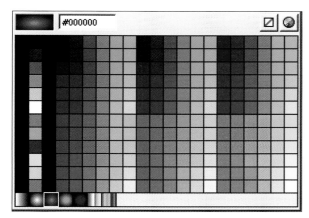

Figure 5.60 Select the pre-set radial fill that is black and red.

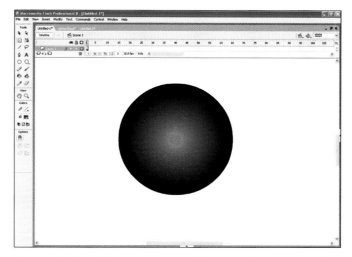

Figure 5.61 The circle you created should have the black and red radial fill you selected.

5. Transforming and Filling Objects

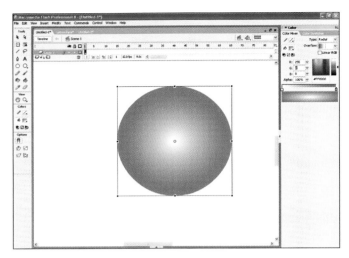

Figure 5.62 You should now have a red circle with a white center.

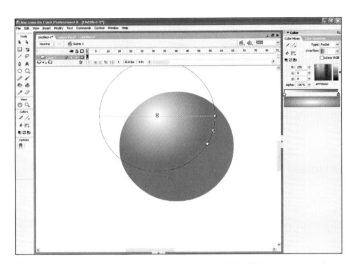

Figure 5.63 After you move the center point of the fill to the top-left corner, you're finished!

9. Type 255 in the R box, and type 0 in the G and B boxes. You should be left with a white and red circle, as shown in Figure 5.62.

10. To move the center point of the fill to the top-left corner, click the Gradient Transform tool and position the mouse pointer over the white circle that appears in the middle of the circle. Then click and drag the center point to the top-left corner, as shown in Figure 5.63. You did it!

Transparencies

In the world of Flash, transparency—or how "see through" an object is—is known as *alpha*. This feature allows you to create animations with objects that fade in and out. You can adjust the alpha level via the Color Mixer.

1. Create and then select any type of shape.

2. If the Color Mixer is not already open, press Shift+F9 to open it.

3. Click the Alpha down arrow to display a slider bar.

4. Drag the slider up or down to adjust the alpha level. The closer you get to 0, the more "see through" your object will be (see Figure 5.64).

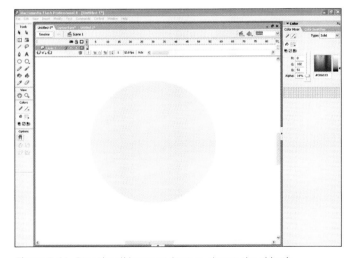

Figure 5.64 Drag the slider up or down to change the object's transparency level.

PRO • FILE

Name: Evan Spiridellis
Organization: JibJab Media Inc.
URL: http://www.jibjab.com

How did you learn Flash? I went to Barnes and Noble and bought a $20 Peach Pit book. I also did the tutorials that come with the program.

How did you get started using Flash? I was developing some ideas with stop-motion photography back in '97–98 when my brother introduced me to the Internet. It was very rudimentary, but we watched John Kricfalusi's, the creator of *Ren and Stimpy*, dancing doodie streaming over a 56K modem and saw an opportunity. Never before had two creators been able to distribute their work to a worldwide audience without the approval or interference of a major media conglomerate. I began to learn Flash because it was the only tool available that would allow us to distribute our work online.

What feature or tool do you use most often? Flash is GREAT for storyboarding and timing. Being able to shift an action a keyframe to the left or right can sometimes be the difference between a joke working and not working. I also draw and paint in Flash with the Paintbrush and Line tools.

What do you like best about Flash? The thing I like best about Flash is being able to watch a project evolve from the rough initial idea into the polished final product, all in one place. In a traditional animation pipeline, all the different aspects of a production are broken up into separate departments. I think having the creator or director's hands on the project all the way through production can only make the final product better. And because it is such a hands-on process, it also means that you can constantly be refining the project until the very last minute.

What sets your animations apart from others? That's a good question.... The only thing I can think of is that we don't really concern ourselves with what other people are doing. We are constantly trying to outdo ourselves and improve what *we* do. Each project is a learning experience, and we're always looking for ways to challenge ourselves.

What is the secret to a great animation? If there's any secret to great animation, it's learning how to draw. After that, it's observing the world around you, studying the old Masters (read the "Illusion of Life"), being passionate about what it is you're working on, and then learning how to draw some more!

Are there any tips that you can share with the readers about using Flash? The only way to get good at anything is by putting in the time. Flash is no different.

Are there any animation tips you can share with our readers? Draw, draw, and then draw some more. Watch the old Disney movies, and then pick up a pencil and draw.

Do you have any other advice for teens getting started with Flash animations? The only other advice I can offer about animation is to have a point of view. When I was in college, I had a teacher who told me to READ EVERYTHING—newspapers, comic books, classic literature, instruction manuals, everything! The more information you have, the more you'll have to say, and the stronger your point of view will be. Good animation is good storytelling, and that all boils down to communication.

Samples

chapter 6
Working with Layers

Have you ever seen how traditional cartoons are made? Different parts of the cartoon are drawn on clear sheets called *cells*, which are all stacked on top of each other to create the entire scene. For example, the background is drawn on one cell, each character is drawn on its own cell, as are different objects. In Flash, *layers* are used in much the same way as cells are used in traditional cartoons. In Flash, you can create as many layers—which are very much like transparent sheets of paper on which you draw your objects—as you like. Layers are then stacked one on top of the other, just like the cells used to create cartoons of old. And because these layers are see-through, you can't distinguish one layer from another when looking at the Stage.

There are several advantages to using layers in Flash. Most importantly, layers help you keep track of the objects in your animations. After all, animations can consist of anywhere from dozens to thousands of objects; using layers, you can organize different categories of objects on different layers. Another advantage of using layers is that objects kept on separate layers don't interact with objects on other layers. When you move an object on one layer on top of an object on another layer, you will still be able to select both objects because they are on separate layers. As a result, you should get in the habit of creating layers for each category of object in your animation. For example, each character should be created on a different layer, the background should be on a separate layer, and comments and sounds should be on layers.

Creating and Naming Layers

Layers are found in the Timeline. By default, one layer is already created for you, but Flash allows you to create as many layers as you like. Creating layers is as simple as clicking a button; after you create a layer, you should name it so that you can easily keep track of it.

1. Start by creating a circle on the Stage using any color fill but with no stroke color. This shape will be created on layer 1, the default layer.

2. Click the New Layer button in the bottom-left corner of the Timeline's Layers area (see Figure 6.1). A new layer, layer 2, will appear, and will be selected.

3. Create a rectangle with any color fill but with no outline color. This rectangle will be created on layer 2, because layer 2 is currently selected.

4. With the Selection tool, click the circle, and then look at the Timeline's Layers area. Layer 1 is now selected because the circle is on layer 1. Next, click the rectangle; you'll notice that layer 2 is now selected.

5. Using the Selection tool, click the rectangle and drag it so that it partially overlaps the circle, as shown in Figure 6.2.

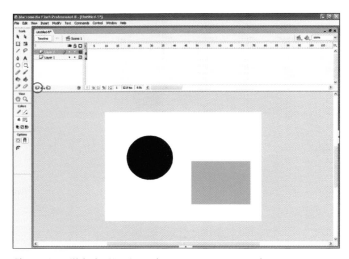

Figure 6.1 Click the New Layer button to create a new layer.

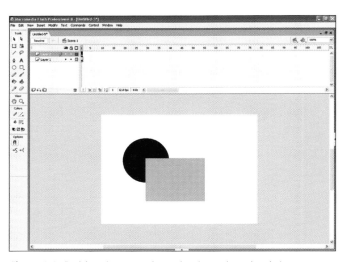

Figure 6.2 Position the rectangle so that it overlaps the circle.

6. Click the circle and drag it to another location on the screen. You'll notice that because the circle is on a separate layer, you can still select it even though the rectangle was placed on top of it (see Figure 6.3).

7. Double-click the name layer 1 in the Timeline. A box will appear around the layer name, and the layer will be highlighted. You can now type a new name for the layer—in this case, name the layer Circle, because it has a circle on it (see Figure 6.4).

8. Repeat step 7 for layer 2, calling it Rectangle. It's always a good idea to name your layers so that keeping track of them is a breeze.

Moving Layers

When you moved the rectangle over the circle in the previous section, you probably noticed that the rectangle landed on top. That's because the Rectangle layer is above the Circle layer in the Layers area of the Timeline. By changing the order of the layers, you can change the order in which objects appear on the Stage.

1. If you deleted the circle and rectangle you created in the last section, go back and re-create them on individual layers. Then position the rectangle over the circle, as shown in Figure 6.5.

2. Click the Circle layer in the Layers area; it will be highlighted to indicate that it is selected.

3. Position the mouse pointer over the page icon to the left of the layer name, click, and drag upward. As you drag, a little line will appear, indicating the new location for the layer. Release the mouse button when the line is above the Rectangle layer. Just as the Circle layer is now above the Rectangle layer in the Layers area, the circle on the Stage will be on top of the rectangle (see Figure 6.6).

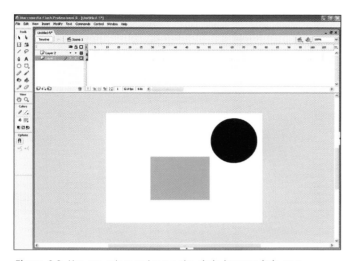

Figure 6.3 You can select and move the circle because it is on a separate layer.

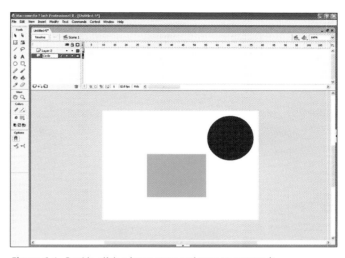

Figure 6.4 Double-click a layer name and type to rename it.

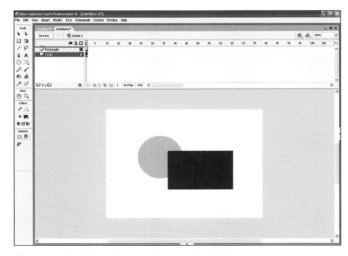

Figure 6.5 Position the rectangle over the circle.

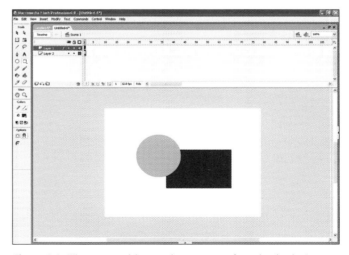

Figure 6.6 When you position one layer on top of another in the Layers area, all the objects on that layer appear on the Stage on top of objects on the layers beneath.

Exploring Layer Features

If you look to the right of the layer name, you'll notice several little icons—typically a pencil, a couple of circles, and a box with a color in it. Each of these icons either indicates something about the layer or allows you to manipulate the layer in some way. For example, you can use these controls to hide a layer, lock a layer, or hide the fills within a layer. Let's look at each of these icons to see how they work:

1. Click a layer in the Timeline's Layers area to select it. (When selecting a layer, it's a good idea to click on the page icon in the layer's bottom-left corner; this will prevent you from inadvertently doing something to the layer.) As soon as the layer is selected, all the objects on the layer will be selected on the Stage, and you should see a pencil icon to the right of the layer name, as shown in Figure 6.7. This pencil icon indicates that that you can draw on or make other changes to objects on that layer.

2. Click the Hide Layer button, which is the dot just to the right of the pencil icon, to hide the contents of your layer. You'll notice that the dot turns into a red ×, and that a red line now appears through the pencil icon to indicate that because the layer is hidden, it can't be edited (see Figure 6.8).

3. To unhide the layer, click the red ×.

4. Click the Lock button, which is the dot just to the left of the colored box in the Timeline's Layers area, to lock the layer. The dot will turn into a little lock icon, and a red line will appear through the pencil icon, as shown in Figure 6.9. When a layer is locked, it is protected against any changes, meaning you can't select or edit any objects on the layer. This feature is particularly useful if you don't want to accidentally move or delete objects on a layer.

5. To unlock the layer, simply click on the lock icon.

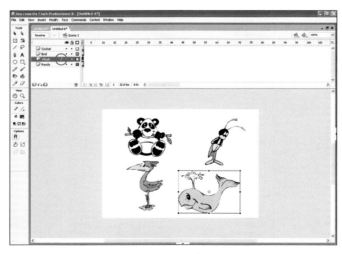

Figure 6.7 Notice the pencil icon beside the layer name; it indicates that the layer is editable.

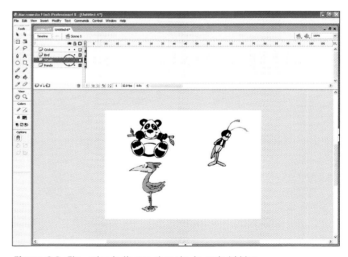

Figure 6.8 The red × indicates that the layer is hidden.

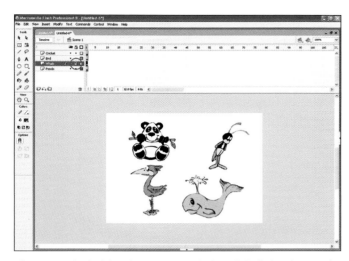

Figure 6.9 The lock icon indicates that the layer is locked and cannot be edited.

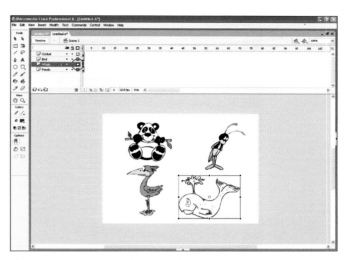

Figure 6.10 By removing the layer's fill, you can see the objects on the layers underneath.

6. Click the colored box to the right of the Lock button (see Figure 6.10); all the fills in the layer will disappear. This feature is great if you have many objects on your layer and want to see the contents of the layers underneath.

7. Click the colored square again; the fill will return.

> To move an object to a different layer, first select the object and press Ctrl+X to cut it. Next, click the layer where you want to place the object and press Ctrl+V to paste the object on that layer.

8. At the top of the Layers area, you'll notice three icons: an eye, a lock, and an outline of a square, as shown in Figure 6.11. Click the eye icon to hide all the layers on the Stage. To unhide the layers, click the eye icon again.

9. Click the lock icon to lock all the layers on the Stage. To unlock the layers, click the lock icon again.

10. Click the square outline to hide the fills of all objects on all layers on the Stage. Click the square outline again to redisplay the fills.

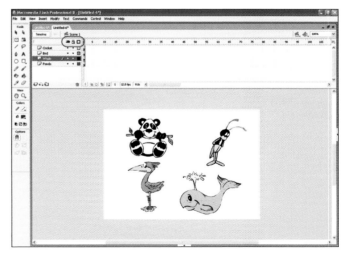

Figure 6.11 You can click these icons to hide, lock, or remove the fills from all the layers at once.

6. Working with Layers

Removing Layers

If you no longer require a layer, you can delete it by selecting the layer in the Layers area and then clicking the trash icon at the bottom of the palette, as shown in Figure 6.12. When you click this button, the layer that is currently selected and all of the objects on that layer will be deleted. You will not be given any warning, so be careful about clicking this button!

Organizing Your Layers in Folders

Just as you use layers to help keep the objects in your animations organized, you can use layer *folders* to keep your layers organized. Using layer folders, you can group related layers together—especially helpful if you have lots of layers to keep track of! Once you have placed a layer or layers into a folder, you can expand or hide the folder as needed. Here's how it works:

1. Create several layers with different names, much like what you see in Figure 6.13.

2. Click the Insert Layer Folder button twice to create two folders in the Layers area, one called Folder 1 and the other called Folder 2. As shown in Figure 6.14, you can rename these folders just as you would rename a layer.

3. Position the mouse pointer over the page icon beside the layer that you want to file in a folder, click, and drag the layer over the desired folder. As shown in Figure 6.15, the folder icon will be highlighted when your mouse pointer is over it; release the mouse button to place the layer in the folder. Repeat this step, placing all your layers in one or the other of the folders you created.

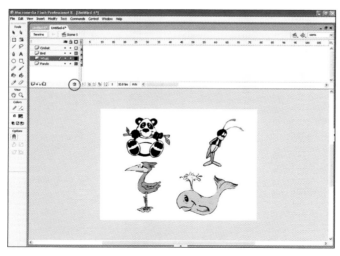

Figure 6.12 Click the Delete Layer button to remove the selected layer and all its contents.

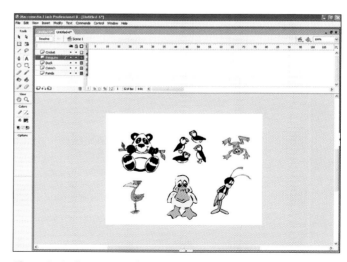

Figure 6.13 Create several layers to place in layer folders.

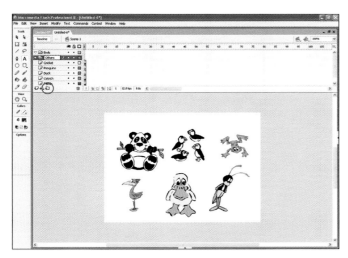

Figure 6.14 When you create new layer folders, they are given default names like Folder 1, Folder 2, and so on. You can rename the folders by double-clicking the folder name and typing a new name.

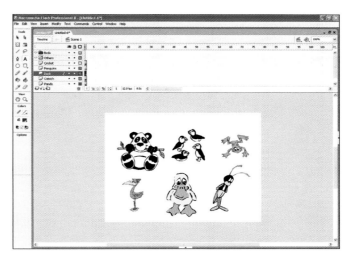

Figure 6.15 Here I moved the Duck layer to the Birds folder. Notice how the icon for the Birds folder becomes dark when the layer is moved over it.

4. Just to the left of the folder icon, you'll see a little triangle pointing downward (see Figure 6.16). This indicates that the folder is expanded—that is, you can see all the layers within it. If you click this triangle, the contents of the folder will no longer be seen, but the layers will still be visible on the Stage. If you click the triangle again, the folder will expand to reveal its contents.

> To remove a layer from a folder, simply click the layer and drag it from inside the folder to any location on the Layers area outside the folder.

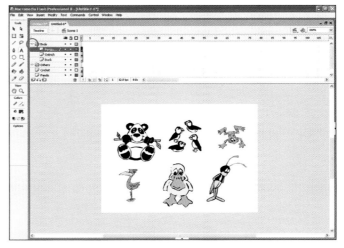

Figure 6.16 You can expand or hide the contents of a folder by clicking the triangle beside the folder name.

Using Guide Layers

In the previous chapter, you learned about the snapping and alignment features, which you can use to align and space objects on the Stage. Guide layers are another way to help you align objects. You can place measurement points such as lines or shapes on a guide layer to help you position your objects on the Stage. Guide layers can also be used as tracing paper—that is, after you create a guide layer, you can import an image or photograph to it and then draw over the imported image on a new layer using the guide layer as a template. Guide layers won't show up in your final animation or in an SWF file (that is, a Flash movie file) if you publish your animation to one.

1. Click the Insert Layer button at the bottom of the Layers area to create a new layer. A new layer will appear.

2. Create any necessary guide shapes on the layer that you just created. You can create any type of shape.

3. Give the guide layer a meaningful name—one that indicates that this layer is a guide layer.

4. Right-click the layer and choose Guide from the menu that appears, as shown in Figure 6.17. The layer will now be a guide layer, as indicated by the small ruler icon that appears.

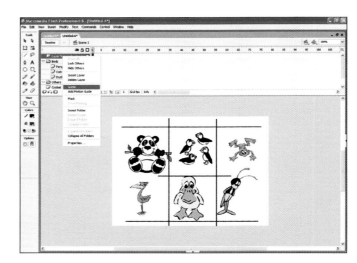

Figure 6.17 Here I created a guide layer with several horizontal and vertical lines, which I can use to position my objects.

OTHER LAYER OPTIONS

A quick way to change several of a layer's options all at once is to double-click the page icon beside the layer's name in the Layers area. This opens the Layer Properties dialog box (see Figure 6.18), which has a variety of settings that you can adjust for your layer. After you've made the changes, click the OK button, and the changes you made will be applied.

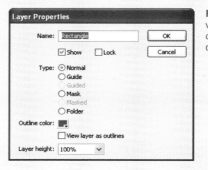

Figure 6.18 You can change various layer options all at once from the Layer Properties dialog box.

chapter 7
Animation 101

This chapter dives into the heart and soul of Flash—which is, of course, animation. Just like in a flipbook, the process of animating your objects in Flash involves having them change in some manner from frame to frame. Animation can consist of a variety of changes to your objects as time passes. For example, your objects can move, change color, change shape, change size, and undergo a variety of other transformations as the animation is played.

There are two methods you can use to animate your objects in Flash: frame by frame and/or tweening. As the name suggests, frame-by-frame animation involves manually changing your objects on the Stage in each frame to create the illusion of movement or to change the attributes of an object over time. With the other method, *tweening*, which is short for "in between," you specify the object's starting point and its end point, and Flash creates all the objects "in between." This chapter explores both of these methods of animation.

Understanding the Timeline

The Timeline that you briefly explored earlier in this book is of vital importance when it comes to animations. As its name suggests, the Timeline represents time as it passes in your animation. When you play your animation, Flash displays the contents of a frame, moving from left to right, across the Timeline. The Timeline is made up of little rectangles, each representing one frame in your animation; the number of frames in the animation is displayed at the top of the Timeline. The red line in the Timeline, called the *playhead*, indicates which frame is currently being displayed on the Stage.

Using the Timeline, you can assign special attributes to your frames, insert frames, change the type of frames, and control the speed at which the animation plays. You can also use the Timeline to create frames, which can be one of three types:

◆ **Keyframe.** *Keyframes* are the cornerstone of animations in Flash. They signify that something has either just been created or has changed. Imagine an animation that included a bird that flew from the left side of the Stage, stopped in the middle of the Stage, and then moved upward. In order to create this type of animation, you would need a keyframe at the point where the bird started; a keyframe in the center, where it changed direction; and a keyframe at the end, where it stopped. Whenever a change occurs in an animation, a keyframe is necessary.

◆ **Static frame.** A *static frame* displays the same content as the frame before it. In many animations, you'll want the action to pause for a moment. To create these pauses, you use static frames.

◆ **Blank keyframe.** A blank keyframe is a completely blank frame in the Timeline.

Each layer that you create will have its own row of frames, which means you can animate objects on different layers independently. For example, say you create a keyframe on a particular layer. That keyframe will be applied to all objects on that layer, but will not affect objects on a different layer. Okay, enough theory, let's get to animating.

Creating Frame-by-Frame Animations

In frame-by-frame animation, you adjust the attributes of your objects—for example, their position, size, and color—on each individual frame of the animation. To accomplish this, you start by creating an object on the first frame (which will become the first keyframe) and then changing that object's attributes in other frames.

1. Start by creating a ball for use in this animation—a circle with a radial gradient fill. (Make sure that the Object Drawing option is selected in the Options section of the Tools panel before you create the circle.) In Figure 7.1 I've created the ball along with a background image.

2. Notice the dot in the first frame of the Timeline. This dot indicates that this frame is a keyframe—in this case, because this is the frame in which the object was created. Position your mouse pointer over frame 2 in the Timeline and click once. You'll notice that frame 2 is now highlighted in blue, as shown in Figure 7.2.

> If you can't remember how to make a circle with a radial gradient fill, refer to Chapter 5, "Transforming and Filling Objects."

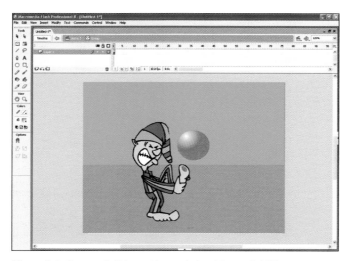

Figure 7.1 Create a ball by making a circle with a radial fill.

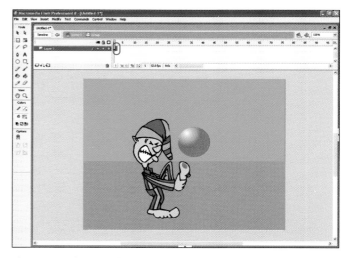

Figure 7.2 When you click a frame in the Timeline, it will be highlighted.

3. Right-click frame 2 and choose Insert Keyframe from the menu that appears, as shown in Figure 7.3. Frame 2 will remain selected, and all the objects in frame 1 will be copied to frame 2.

4. Right now, your ball and any background content you added are in both frame 1 and frame 2, in the exact same position. Because frame 2 is now a keyframe, you can change the position of the ball in that frame without affecting its position in frame 1. Using the Selection tool, move the ball in frame 2 slightly to the right, as shown in Figure 7.4.

5. Press the Enter or Return key on your keyboard to play your animation. You'll notice that the sphere quickly moves from left to right. Wow! Your first frame-by-frame animation! That wasn't so hard was it? Let's continue the animation by repeating step 4 for the next three frames. When you're finished and you play your animation, the ball should move from one side of the Stage to the other.

Creating Multiple Keyframes

In the animation you just created, you created your keyframes one at a time. To save yourself some time, you can create many keyframes at once. In this example I've used an image of a car moving across a background, but you can create the effect with any object.

1. Create an image in the first frame of the animation. A keyframe will automatically be created in that frame, because it is the first frame that contains the image.

2. Click and drag across the frames in the Timeline that you would like to convert to keyframes. When you release the mouse button, they will all be highlighted, indicating that they have been selected.

3. Right-click any of these selected frames and choose Convert to Keyframes from the menu that appears (see Figure 7.5). All the selected frames will now be keyframes, and the object that you placed in the initial frame will be copied to each selected frame.

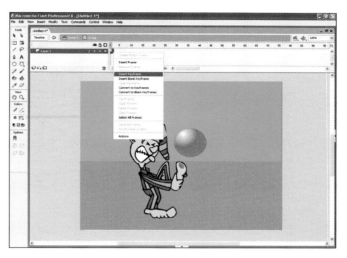

Figure 7.3 Insert a keyframe in frame 2.

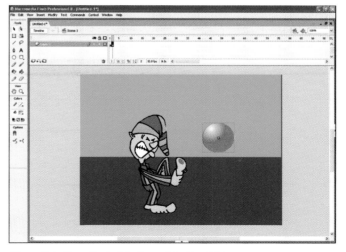

Figure 7.4 Move the ball in frame 2 to the right.

7. Animation 101

101

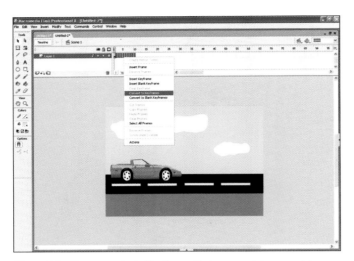

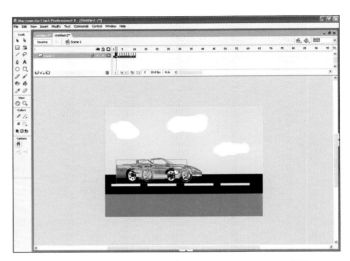

Figure 7.5 After you selecte the frames that you want to convert to keyframes, right-click them and choose Convert to Keyframes.

Figure 7.6 By creating multiple keyframes at once, you can quickly create frame-by-frame animations. Here you move your object to the right slightly in each frame.

4. Click frame 2 in the Timeline to select it.

5. On the Stage, move the object in frame 2—in this case, the car—slightly to the right, as shown in Figure 7.6.

6. Repeat this step for the rest of the keyframes, moving the object progressively farther to the right.

7. Press the Enter or Return key on your keyboard to play the animation and watch your object move across the screen.

Adding, Copying, and Pasting Frames

Earlier, you created an animation that had only two frames. Most animations that you create, however, will have dozens, if not hundreds of frames. In this section, you'll create a pair of cartoon eyes that consist of two eyeballs and two pupils, and then generate a frame-by-frame animation with many different frames to move the pupils around. In the process, you'll learn to add frames, as well as copy and paste them—which is useful when you want to repeat actions in your animations without having to re-create them.

1. Start by creating a new Flash animation that contains eyeballs and pupils, as shown in Figure 7.7. (I've created an entire face here, but for this exercise, you need only create the eyes.) The eyeballs are ovals with radial gradient fills, and the pupils are simply smaller black circles. Make sure that the Object Drawing option is selected in the Options section of the Tools panel before you create the circles.

2. While pressing the Shift key, use the Selection tool to click both of the pupils.

3. With both pupils selected, press Ctrl+G to group them together. That way, you can animate them both at the same time.

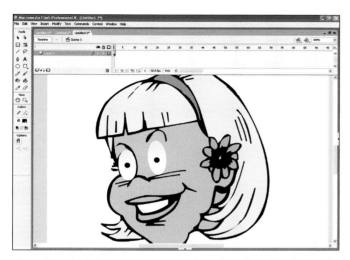

Figure 7.7 Create two cartoon eyes, as shown here, by making two ovals and two circles.

Figure 7.8 By positioning the pupils all the way to the left of the eyeballs, you create the illusion of movement.

4. Right-click frame 5 in layer 1 and choose Insert Keyframe from the menu that appears. (You are choosing frame 5 because you don't want the action to happen instantly; rather, you want a little bit of a pause before you make the pupils move.) The eyeballs and pupils will be copied on every frame between frames 1 and 5. You will also now have a keyframe on frame 5, where you can adjust the position of the pupils without affecting their position on any of the previous frames.

5. When you create a keyframe, all the objects on that layer will be selected. Click any blank area of the Stage to deselect the objects.

6. Click and drag the pupils all the way to the left of the eyeballs, as shown in Figure 7.8. This will make the pupils move when the object is animated.

7. Press the Enter or Return key on your keyboard to play the animation that you've created so far. You should see that after a third of a second, the pupils jump from the center of the eyes to the left.

8. Next, you'll get the pupils to jump back to the center of the eye after another third of a second goes by. To begin, right-click frame 10 in layer 1 and choose Insert Keyframe from the menu that appears.

> When you create a keyframe, all the objects in the previous keyframe get copied onto the frames in between. For example, if you create a circle on frame 1 and then create a keyframe on frame 100, every frame between frames 1 and 100 would also contain that circle. Because there is no action in these frames, when you play the animation, it will appear as though nothing is happening, or that the action is paused. The number of frames between the two keyframes will determine the length of this pause.

7. Animation 101

9. Now click in any blank area of the Stage to deselect the objects.

10. Position the pupils back in the center of the eyes, and then press the Enter or Return key to watch the animation that you've created up to this point. What you should see now are the pupils moving left and then back to the center.

11. Say you want to lengthen the time between the pupils moving. In other words, rather than having the pupils move after only a moment, you want the pupils to start in middle, stay there for three seconds, and then move to the left, where they'll remain for three more seconds before moving back to the center. To accomplish this, you simply need to add frames between the keyframes you created earlier. To begin, click any frame on your Timeline between the first keyframe (frame 1) and the second keyframe (currently frame 5). The frame you click will be highlighted, as shown in Figure 7.9.

12. Press the F5 key about 30 times. Each time you press F5, one additional frame will be added to the Timeline. You should notice that as you add frames, the keyframes after the selected frame are moving farther down the Timeline. Each of the frames that you add will be static frames, and will contain the objects that were on the keyframe before them.

13. Select any frame between the second and last keyframe, and repeat step 12 to insert additional frames (see Figure 7.10). Your Timeline should now be quite a bit longer. Press the Enter or Return key to watch your animation; you should notice that the pupils pause in each of their new locations a lot longer than before.

Figure 7.9 Select any frame between frame 1 and frame 5. When selected, the frame is highlighted.

Figure 7.10 By inserting additional frames between keyframes, you increase the time that the action pauses.

14. The next step of your animation is to have the pupils move in the other direction. Right now, they move from the center to the left, and then back to the center. You want to add more frames so that after the pupils move back to the center, they will move to the right and then back again. Rather than having to re-create these movements and make all new keyframes, however, you can copy and paste your existing frames. To begin, position your mouse pointer over frame 1 in the Timeline, click, and drag to the right until the last keyframe is highlighted, as shown in Figure 7.11. All the frames in your animation are now selected. (Another way to select all the frames in your animation is to press Ctrl+Alt+A.)

15. Open the Edit menu, choose Timeline, and select Copy Frames. The frames that you selected will be copied to the system clipboard and can now be pasted elsewhere.

16. Click the first blank frame, which is directly after the last keyframe in the Timeline, as shown in Figure 7.12.

17. Open the Edit menu, choose Timeline, and select Paste Frames to paste all the frames you had on the clipboard into the Timeline.

18. If you played the animation now, you'd see the pupils looking to the left twice. You need to change the second instance of the pupils moving to the left so that they are moving to the right. To begin, click the keyframe in the Timeline that begins the second instance of the pupils moving to the left and drag to the right to select the frames.

Figure 7.11 You can select the frames in your Timeline by clicking and dragging across them.

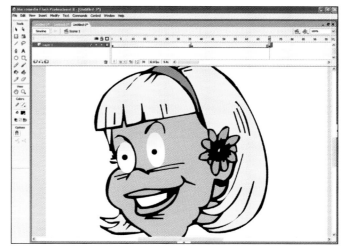

Figure 7.12 Click the first empty frame in your animation; that's where you paste the frames currently on the clipboard.

7. Animation 101

105

19. Click on the frame that contains the second-to-last keyframe. Because all the objects on the Stage are still selected, you'll need to click any blank area to deselect them. Then click and drag the pupils to the right side of the eyeballs, as shown in Figure 7.13. Just changing this one keyframe changes the direction of the pupils' movement.

20. Press Ctrl+Alt+R to move the playhead to the beginning of your animation, and then press the Enter or Return key on your keyboard. What you should see are the pupils starting in the center, moving to the left, returning to the center, moving to the right, and then going back to the center. By adding frames, copying, and pasting, you've managed to create pauses and extend your animation.

Figure 7.13 Move the pupils to the right in the second-to-last keyframe.

Removing and Clearing Frames

Flash gives you several options for getting rid of content in your animations. To clear or remove frames, do the following:

1. Select the frames in the Timeline that you want to clear or remove by clicking and dragging across them.

2. Right-click the selection or an individual frame and choose Clear Frames or Remove Frames from the menu that appears to remove objects from the selected frame but leave the frame in place or to remove the frame and all of its contents, respectively.

So far, we've stuck to using movement for your frame-by-frame animations, but don't think that's all you can do! In addition to moving elements frame by frame, you can do all sorts of other wonderful things to your objects, including changing their colors, reshaping them, or replacing them with other objects.

Using Flash's Onion Skin Feature

So far, when you've created your frame-by-frame animations, you've simply roughly moved your shapes around. Rather than having to guess where to move objects on the Stage when creating animations, however, you can use the Onion Skin feature to help you get an understanding of what's going on in your animation before and after your current frame. The Onion Skin feature makes your frames partially see-through so that you can tell what happened in the frame or frames before and after. (This feature is called "Onion Skin" because actual onion skin is partially see-through and layered, not unlike the frames in Flash.)

1. Create an object and use it to make a frame-by-frame animation on the first 10 frames of your Timeline, moving the object to different locations on the Stage in each frame. For example, have your object move from left to right across the Stage.

2. Click frame 5.

3. Click the Onion Skin button. In addition to seeing your object at its position in frame 5, you should see a translucent view of the object's position in a few of the frames before and after the current frame (see Figure 7.14). You can now move your object around precisely, knowing exactly where your object will be in relation to the objects in the frames before and after it.

4. If you take a close look at the Timeline header, you'll notice two interesting shapes surrounding the currently selected frames. These shapes indicate the number of frames you can see through. To increase or decrease the number of frames that show through, position your mouse pointer over one of these shapes and click and drag inward (toward the playhead) or outward to decrease or increase the number of frames that show through, respectively (see Figure 7.15).

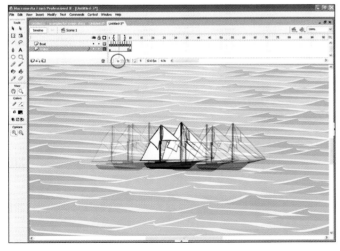

Figure 7.14 Click the Onion Skin button to see some of the frames before and after the current frame.

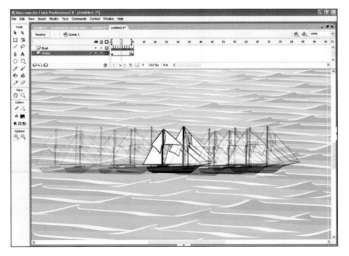

Figure 7.15 You can drag the Start Onion Skin and End Onion Skin markers to adjust how many frames are shown.

7. Animation 101

107

In addition to using the Onion Skin feature to track your animation over several frames at once, you can use it to trace objects. This is particularly useful if you want to trace a photograph. Simply place the photograph on one frame and turn the Onion Skin feature on in the next frame. You can now trace the image, as shown in Figure 7.16, and then delete the first frame.

Onion Skin Options

You can control a variety of options for Flash's Onion Skin feature. Click the Modify Onion Markers button to display a menu of options (see Figure 7.17):

◆ **Always Show Markers.** Select this option to always show the Onion Skin markers, regardless of whether the Onion Skin feature is turned on or not.

◆ **Anchor Onion.** This setting locks the markers in their current location so that they cannot be moved. To turn this feature off, click this option in the menu again to deselect it.

◆ **Anchor 2.** This setting places the Start Onion Skin and End Onion Skin markers two frames before and after the current frame, respectively.

◆ **Anchor 5.** This setting places the Start Onion Skin and End Onion Skin markers five frames before and after the current frame, respectively.

◆ **Onion All.** This setting positions the Start Onion Skin and End Onion Skin markers around the first and last frame of your animation.

> The marker positions for the Onion Skin are relative to the current frame. That means that you'll have to set the markers individually for each frame.

Figure 7.16 You can use the Onion Skin feature to trace an image.

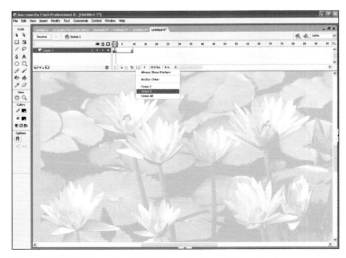

Figure 7.17 Clicking the Modify Onion Markers button displays a menu with different options for this feature.

Reversing Frames

The ability to reverse frames can be a huge time-saver in Flash. For example, imagine you've created an animation of a ball flying up in the air. Rather than having to create the frames for the ball falling back down to Earth, you can copy the original frames, paste them, and then reverse them. Reversing a selection of frames switches them around so that the last frame appears first and the first frame appears last. Sound confusing? It isn't really, just follow these steps:

1. Create a frame-by-frame animation that contains half the action you want to include—for example, a ball moving upward, eyes moving in one direction, or a character jumping. The example I use here shows a frame-by-frame animation with four frames of a seal that has a ball moving upward.

2. Click and drag across the frames that include the animation you want to reverse in order to select them.

3. Open the Edit menu, choose Timeline, and select Copy Frames to copy the selected frames, as shown in Figure 7.18.

4. Click the first empty frame in the Timeline and then open the Edit menu, choose Timeline, and select Paste Frames, as shown in Figure 7.19. The copied frames will be pasted into your Timeline, the result being that your animation will basically repeat itself. Your next step is to reverse the frames you just pasted.

5. Click and drag across the frames that you just pasted in order to select them.

6. Open the Modify menu, choose Timeline, and select Reverse Frames to reverse the frames.

7. Press Enter or Return to play the animation. You should notice that the frames you pasted play in reverse.

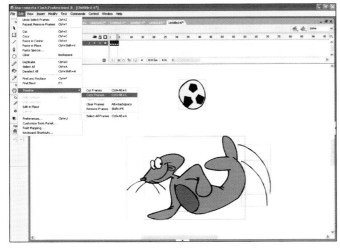

Figure 7.18 Copy the frames that include the animation that you want to reverse.

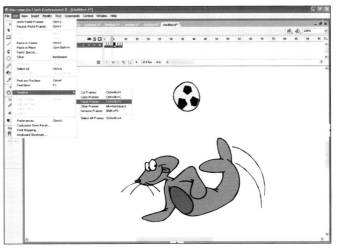

Figure 7.19 Paste the copied frames into the Timeline. The Timeline should look like this when you are finished.

7. Animation 101

Tweening

Imagine that you want to create a five-minute animation. Using Flash's default settings, you'd have to create more than 3,500 frames. Although you *could* create this type of animation frame-by-frame, why would you want to? The folks who developed Flash understand this, which is why they give you the option of using tweening. *Tweening* allows you to create a starting point and an ending point for an object, and let Flash create all the objects in between. Believe me, once you really get into animating, tweening will be your new best friend because it will save you so much time. Even if you were making a simple animation—of, say, a tire moving across the Stage for several seconds—using the frame-by-frame technique would require you to manipulate more than a dozen frames, one by one. By using tweening, however, you would need to adjust only two frames—the one that represented the tire's starting point and the one that represented its end point.

Motion Tweening

The first type of tweening this chapter is going to explore is *motion tweening*. With this type of tweening, you can use just a few clicks of the mouse button to create an object and have it move to a new location on the Stage; Flash will do the rest.

1. On a separate layer in the first frame, create the object you want to animate.

2. Press Ctrl+F3 to open the Property inspector if it is not already open.

3. I want to make this animation 20 frames long. To do so, right-click frame 20 in the same layer and select Insert Keyframe from the menu that appears. The shape you created will be copied to all the frames after frame 1 up to frame 20.

4. Click frame 1. Then, in the Property inspector, open the Tween drop-down menu and select Motion, as shown in Figure 7.20. Believe it or not, you've just created a motion tween—although if you ran the animation now, nothing would happen because you haven't moved the object to its end point yet. Once you've selected the Motion option, an arrow will appear in the Timeline between the first and last frames.

5. Click frame 20 and move your object to another location on the Stage.

6. Press the Enter or Return key to play the animation; the object will move across the Stage, starting at its position in frame 1 and ending at its position in frame 20 (see Figure 7.21). Isn't motion tweening great? In just a few steps you can make objects fly across the Stage!

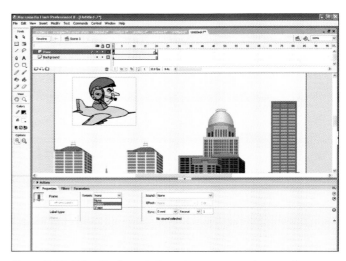

Figure 7.20 Using the Property inspector, you can assign a motion tween. (By the way, for this series, I created a background on a separate layer and copied it to all the frames; feel free to do the same if you're so inclined.)

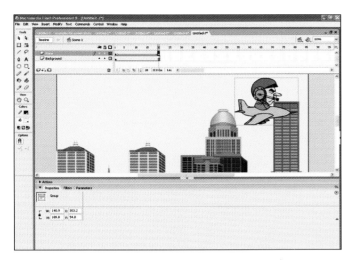

Figure 7.21 After you move the object in the final frame of the animation, your motion tween will be complete.

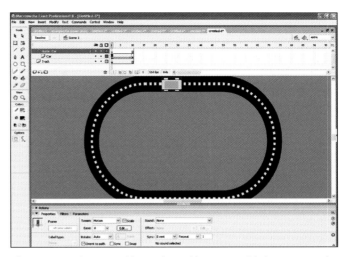

Figure 7.22 When you add a motion guide, a new guide layer appears in the Layers area.

Using the Orient to Path Option

In the motion tween you created in the last section, the object moved in a straight line from its original position to the position where you moved it. Most objects in real life, however, don't travel in a straight path. Consider a bird, for instance—birds don't typically fly in a straight line. Likewise, if you wanted to create an animation of a bird, you'd want it to fly to different locations on the screen, in all different directions. To achieve that effect, you can use the Orient to Path option. The same goes for a car on an oval track—you'd want to circle the track rather than simply drive in a straight line. To dictate an object's path, do the following:

1. Start by creating a motion tween, as you did in the preceding section.

2. Click the frame where the animation starts.

3. In the Property inspector, click the Orient to Path checkbox to select it.

4. In the Layers area on the Timeline, click the Add Motion Guide button. A motion guide will be added to this layer, and will appear as a guide layer in the Layers area (see Figure 7.22).

7. Animation 101

111

5. Click the Pencil tool and draw a path on the Stage; your animation will move along the path you draw. (Note that you could also use the Pen, Line, Circle, Rectangle, or Brush tool here.) You can make this path a curved or squiggly line, or even a shape or pattern. In this example, shown in Figure 7.23, I drew a path that goes around a track. (My path is red, but it really doesn't matter what color you make your path because you will hide it in the following steps.

6. Click the Selection tool and move the object so that it is centered on the start of the path, as shown in Figure 7.24.

7. Click the last frame of the motion tween.

8. Position the object on the last frame so that it is centered on the end of the path, as shown in Figure 7.25.

9. Click the guide layer's Hide Layer button to hide the path, as shown in Figure 7.26. (Even if you don't hide the path, it won't appear in your final exported animation.)

10. Press the Enter or Return key to play the animation. The object will follow along the path as the animation plays.

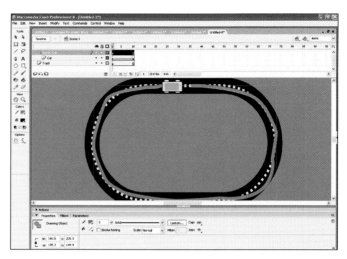

Figure 7.23 You can create any type of path for your motion tween, including lines and shapes.

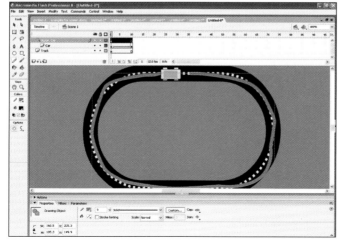

Figure 7.24 Position the object so that it's centered on the beginning of the line.

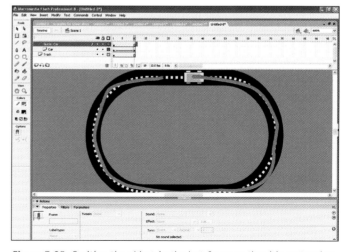

Figure 7.25 Position the object in the last frame so that it's centered at the end of the path.

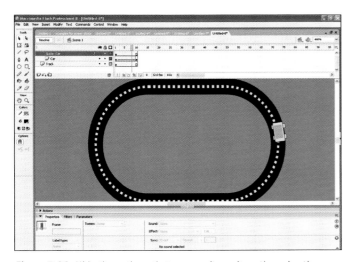

Figure 7.26 Hide the path so that you won't see it as the animation plays.

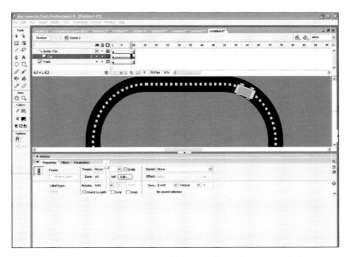

Figure 7.27 You can use the Ease slider to adjust the speed of the animation at the beginning or end of the tween.

Using Flash's Ease Function

Visualize a sprinter running a 100-meter race. When the starting gun fires, the sprinter explodes out of the blocks and increases his speed until he maxes out, maintaining this maximum speed until he crosses the finish line. Then, after he crosses the finish line, the sprinter slows down until he stops. All this is to say that the sprinter's speed changes at the beginning and at the end of the race. That's pretty much how the Ease feature works in Flash. With this feature, you can increase the speed of the animation of the object to be faster at the beginning and/or at the end of the animation.

To use this feature, first create an animation using a motion tween. When you do, you'll notice an Ease drop-down arrow in the Property inspector. Click it to display a slider bar that you can drag up or down to increase or decrease the Ease level respectively, as in Figure 7.27. A higher Ease value makes the object travel more quickly at the beginning of the animation, and a lower value speeds the object up at the end of the animation.

7. Animation 101

113

Rotating Your Animation

Not only can you make objects move from one location to another using the motion tween, you can make objects rotate as they move across the Stage. Here's how it's done:

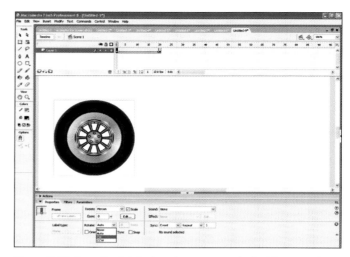

1. After creating a motion tween, click the first frame and open the Rotate drop-down arrow in the Property inspector. As shown in Figure 7.28, a variety of options from which you can choose will appear, including the following:

   ◆ **None.** If this option is selected, no rotation will occur.

   ◆ **Auto.** If this option is selected, the object will rotate once as it moves.

   ◆ **CW.** If this option is selected, the object will rotate in a clockwise direction.

   ◆ **CCW.** If this option is selected, the object will rotate in a counter-clockwise direction.

Figure 7.28 Open the Rotate drop-down menu and select from a variety of rotation options.

2. Type the number of times you want the object to rotate in the Times box. (This option is only available if you select the CW or CCW option.)

3. Press the Enter or Return key and watch your object rotate as it moves across the screen.

Rather than pressing Enter or Return to play your animations in order to preview the changes you have made, you can drag the red playhead in the Timeline. As you drag the playhead forward or backward, the frames will change on the Stage, allowing you to preview your animation.

Shape Tweening

The shape tweening feature allows you to change an object's shape over time without having to edit the shape frame by frame. Using shape tweening, you create a starting object and an ending object, and Flash creates all the transitional shapes in between. This is particularly useful for animating facial expressions, moving body parts, and morphing objects. In this example, I'll show you how to morph a circle into an interesting shape. As it morphs, we'll also move the shape and change its color. Here's how it's done:

1. Make sure the Object Drawing option is enabled. If it is not, press the J key on your keyboard to enable it.

2. Draw a circle of any color on the Stage in frame 1 and position it on the left side of the Stage, as shown in Figure 7.29.

3. Right-click frame 20 and select Insert Keyframe from the menu that appears. You now have a 20-frame animation with no action—yet.

4. Click frame 1, open the Tween drop-down menu in the Property inspector, and select Shape, as shown in Figure 7.30.

5. Click frame 20 and then click the Subselection tool to activate it.

6. Click the circle and drag it to another location on the Stage.

7. Click the circle's outline to display anchor points that you can use to reshape the circle.

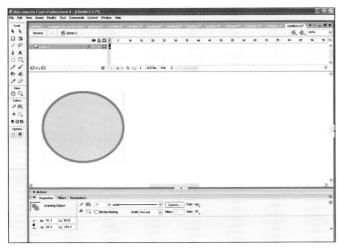

Figure 7.29 You are going to transform this circle using a shape tween.

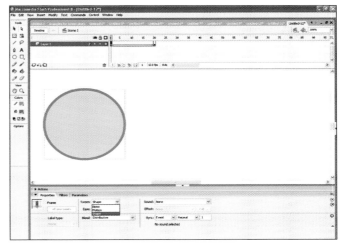

Figure 7.30 Create a shape tween by selecting Shape from the Tween drop-down menu in the Property inspector.

7. Animation 101

8. Click and drag on any of these anchor points to give the circle a new shape.

9. Apply a new fill color to the shape. The shape that you end up with is what the object will morph into when the animation plays (see Figure 7.31).

10. Press the Enter or Return key to play the animation. You should notice that the circle morphs into the interesting shape that you created.

> If you want to remove a shape tween or motion tween from your animation, right-click any frame within the tween and choose Remove Tween from the menu that appears.

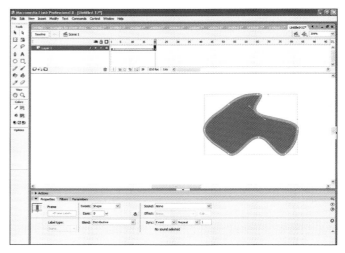

Figure 7.31 By adjusting the object's shape in the last frame of the shape tween, you specify what the object will morph into.

Now You Try

Try to create an animation that has a cartoon face going from happy to sad, as in Figures 7.32 and 7.33. If you get stuck, follow the steps in this section to see how this is done.

1. Create a cartoon character similar to the one you see in Figure 7.32, but leave out the mouth. I used the Pencil tool, Brush tool, and Paint Bucket tool to create my character. Don't worry if your character doesn't look exactly like this one; just try to get close.

2. Rename the layer with the cartoon character "Background" to help keep things organized.

3. Create a new layer and call it "Smile."

4. On the Smile layer, use the Pencil tool to create the character's smile, as shown in Figure 7.34. (Make sure that you create the smile on its own layer—this is very important. If you don't, you can create a real mess, as you'll see in the next section. Also, be sure to draw the smile with the Pencil tool.)

5. Right-click frame 15 in the Background layer and choose Insert Frame from the menu that appears. Notice that you are not creating a keyframe, just a regular frame. You don't need a keyframe because you won't be changing the background at all during the animation. The background you created will be copied to every frame in your animation, ending with frame 15.

Figure 7.32 The cartoon's face should start off smiling.

Figure 7.33 Through shape tweening, you'll turn the smile into a frown over 15 frames. The beauty of this technique is that you'll need to change the smile only on one frame—the last one. Flash will do the rest!

7. Animation 101

117

6. Click the Smile layer to select it.

7. Right-click frame 15 and choose Insert Keyframe from the menu that appears. The smile you created will be copied to every frame in your animation, ending with frame 15.

8. Click frame 1 in the Smile layer to select it. Then, in the Property inspector, open the Tween drop-down menu and select Shape, as shown in Figure 7.35. The smile is now a shape tween.

9. Click frame 15 in the Timeline and use the Free Transform tool to select the smile. A series of handles will appear around the smile.

10. Position the mouse pointer just outside any of the corner handles until the mouse pointer changes into a circle with an arrow, click, and drag until the circle rotates into a frown.

11. The frown will be off center, so click the smile and drag it to the middle of the face, as shown in Figure 7.36.

12. That's it! You've completed your animation. Just press the Enter or Return key and watch the smile morph into a frown.

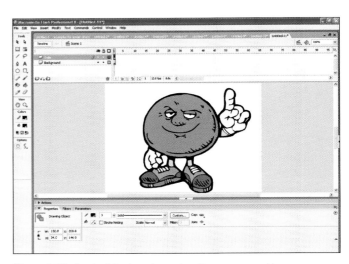

Figure 7.34 Create this character and smile or a reasonable copy.

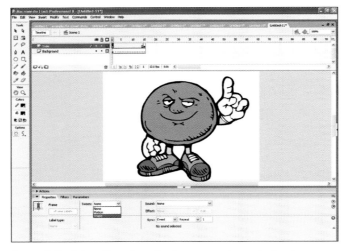

Figure 7.35 Select Shape from the Tween menu to create the shape tween.

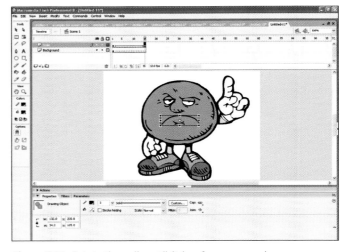

Figure 7.36 Rotate the smile until it is a frown as seen here.

Shape Tweening Different Shapes

When you first created a shape tween you created an image in the first frame and then altered it slightly for the last frame. With shape tweening you can create more outrageous morphs, involving two completely different shapes. In this example I'll make a caterpillar turn into a butterfly using a shape tween, but you can create any type of object.

1. Create an object for the first frame of your shape tween. In this case, I created a caterpillar, as shown in Figure 7.37.

2. Right-click frame 10 and choose Insert Keyframe from the menu that appears. You'll now see the caterpillar on this frame, and it will be selected. Press the Delete key on your keyboard to remove the caterpillar.

3. Create or import another object onto this frame. In this case, I copied a butterfly onto the frame, as shown in Figure 7.38.

4. Click the first frame, open the Tween drop-down menu in the Property inspector, and select Shape, as shown in Figure 7.39.

5. Play your animation. You'll see your object transform. In this case, the caterpillar morphs into a butterfly.

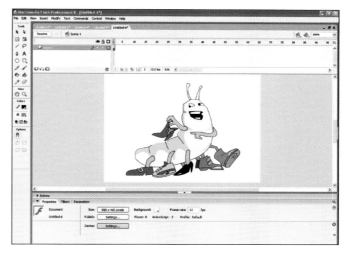

Figure 7.37 Create your object in the first frame.

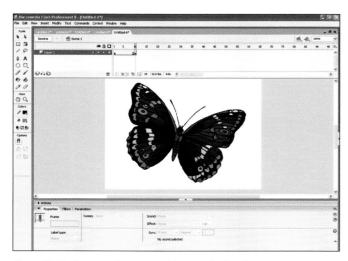

Figure 7.38 Create or import an object on the last frame.

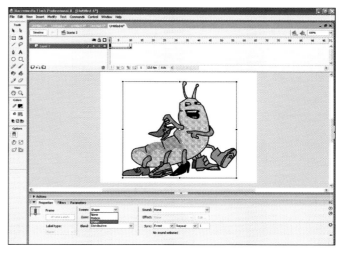

Figure 7.39 After you select Shape from the Tween drop-down menu, the caterpillar will morph into a butterfly when the animation is played.

7. Animation 101

Using Shape Hints

If you play around with shape tweening, you may notice that the transition from one shape to another sometimes gets a little jumbled in the middle, or that it may not go exactly as you expected. To help you control how one shape transitions to another, you can use shape hints. *Shape hints* allow you to specify start points and end points for particular parts of a shape. This is especially useful for facial expressions in cartoons, for moving arms and legs, and for opening and closing mouths. Shape hints are also useful if you want certain objects to stay in place during the transition. To use shape hints, you place a shape hint in the start frame and then match it with a shape hint in the end frame.

1. Create a shape tween. In this example, I've created two simple characters figure skating.

2. When I play this animation, I notice that the animation seems jumbled in the middle frames, as shown in Figure 7.40.

3. Click the first keyframe of your shape tween to select it.

4. Open the Modify menu, choose Shape, and select Add Shape Hint. (Alternatively, press Ctrl+Shift+H.) A red dot will appear on the Stage with the letter "a" in it, indicating the presence of a shape hint.

5. Click and drag this shape hint to the first point on the shape that you would like to mark. In this example, I put the first marker on top of the figure skater's head, as shown in Figure 7.41. I chose the top of the skater's head because when I played the animation, the head got jumbled in the frames in between.

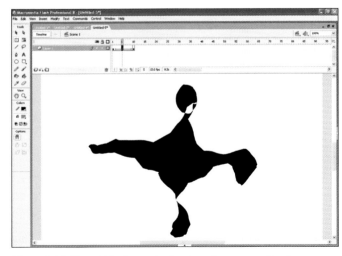

Figure 7.40 The middle frames in the shape tween can often become jumbled.

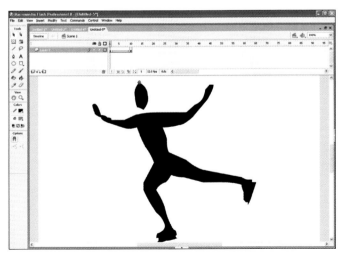

Figure 7.41 Position the first marker at the point where you would like to add a shape hint.

6. Click the last frame of the shape tween. You'll notice that the red dot also appears on this last frame with a corresponding letter "a" in it. Position the red dot at the point in the shape corresponding to the first "a" marker, as shown in Figure 7.42.

7. Click the first frame of your shape tween. You'll notice that the marker is now yellow. If you again clicked the last frame of the animation, you would notice that the marker is now green.

8. Repeat steps 3–6 for other locations on the shape, as shown in Figure 7.43. For example, put a marker on each hand, each foot, and in the middle of the shape. Each marker you create will be assigned a new letter so that you can match the marker on the first frame of the shape hint with the marker on the last frame. You can create up to 26 markers—one for each letter of the alphabet.

> You don't have to create a marker in the first frame and then position it in the last frame one at a time. To save time, you can create all your markers in the first frame and then move to the last frame and position them all.

9. Play the animation; you'll see a much smoother transition.

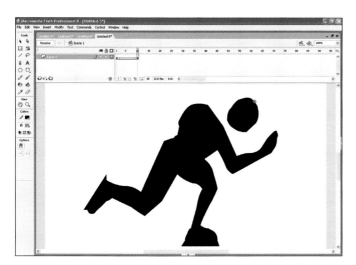

Figure 7.42 Position the marker in the last frame at the spot corresponding with the first marker—in this case, the top of the head.

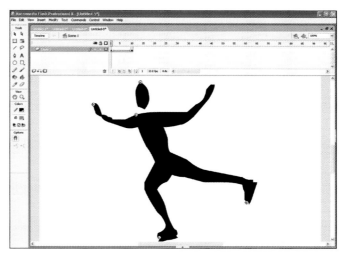

Figure 7.43 Add other shape hints to your shape as seen here.

Shape Tweening Options

If you click any frame in a shape tween, you'll notice that several options appear in the Property inspector. One of these options, Ease, you've already explored. The other option, Blend, controls the process of the transition.

If you open the Blend drop-down menu, you'll notice two options:

- ◆ **Distributive.** This option creates an animation in which the shapes between the first and last frame are irregular.
- ◆ **Angular.** This option creates an animation that keeps the straight lines and corners of the shapes between the first and last frame.

The difference between these blending options can be very subtle, so experiment with both to see which works best for you.

Timing

The whole process of animating involves showing a frame for a specific period of time (usually just a split second) before the next frame is displayed. The quicker a frame is displayed, the faster the animation will be. Flash allows you to control the timing of your animations to speed them up or slow them down. Be aware, however, that you can have only one frame rate for your entire animation. In other words, you can't have it go faster or slower at different points (although there are animation tools you can use to make it *seem* like it's going faster or slower).

1. Create any kind of animation and click any frame within the animation.

2. Look at the bottom of the Timeline; you'll notice three numbers, as shown in Figure 7.44. The first number indicates your current frame, the second number is the speed of your animation represented in fps (frames per second), and the last number indicates how much time has elapsed.

3. The default number for your frame speed 12fps, which is ideal for animations made for the Internet. You can, however, change this number. To begin, open the Document Properties dialog box by displaying the Modify menu and choosing Document.

4. In the Document Properties dialog box, adjust the value in the Frame Rate field to change the fps, as shown in Figure 7.45.

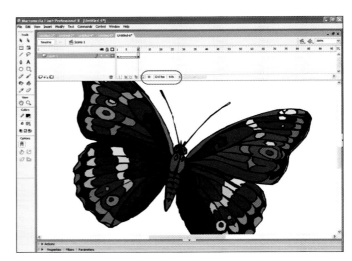

Figure 7.44 The three numbers in the bottom of the Timeline indicate different aspects of the timing of your frame.

Figure 7.45 The Document Properties dialog box allows you to change the frame speed for your animations.

PRO • FILE

Name: David Brown
Organization: AgencyNet Interactive
URL: http://www.agencynet.com

How did you learn Flash? I was a student at The Art Institute of Ft. Lauderdale, but most of my learning was done through personal research and study.

How did you get started using Flash? My beginnings with Flash occurred in school. I then took it upon myself to go beyond the curriculum and learn about dynamic data and how it works within Flash.

What feature or tool do you use most often? I utilize the organizational tools in Flash the most. Creating and naming folders and layers is very important when working with larger, more complex Flash files. It is also important to maintain an organized library when working with a team.

What do you like best about Flash? It's the only program/platform in the world that allows for the seamless integration of audio, video, data, 3D, animations, and true two-way user interactivity. You can create virtually anything you can imagine. The ability to load and utilize external content, be it an image file or data, is another great feature in Flash.

What sets your animations apart from others? With my animations, special consideration is given to the format and size of what is to be animated. Moving or animating objects on the screen via ActionScript rather than the Timeline can produce smoother visual results.

ActionScript is an ECMAScript-based programming language used for controlling Macromedia Flash movies and applications. Because both ActionScript and JavaScript are based on the same ECMAScript syntax, fluency in one easily translates to the other. However, the client model is dramatically different: While JavaScript deals with windows, documents, and forms, ActionScript deals with movie clips, text fields, and sounds.

What is the secret to a great animation? The secret to great animation is a great story. Flash can enable you to tell a great story through animation, but without a good foundation, no amount of technology will help you. There are many different types of animation effects such as frame tweening, multi-layered movement, background animations, and my favorite, trick animations. Trick animation involves using still imagery, with quick cuts of images to give the illusion of speed and drama. A good example of this can be seen in the cartoon series *Teen Titans* or *Dexter's Laboratory*. Oh yeah, and lots of pre-planning prior to executing.

Are there any tips that you can share with the readers about using Flash? Do the tutorials and garner a general knowledge of the program. A Flash user can be a designer, a programmer, an animator or an A/V person. The program is segmented as such. Pick an area that interests you the most and conquer it first. That said, do try to obtain general knowledge of the other parts of Flash that may not be as interesting because it will help to build your overall skill set. Also, assign types to all your variables. When debugging, having your variable types defined will help you immensely.

Are there any animation tips you can share with our readers? There are many different types of animation, as I stated above. Today, many developers use ActionScript code to move elements around the Flash environment. Frame tweens can be a great enhancement to your animations as well. My advice would be to explore the space—start with a basic story and see how you can use a combination of code-based animations and tween-based animations, and you will quickly find the method that works best for you.

Do you have any other advice for teens getting started with Flash animations? My biggest piece of advice is to EXPERIMENT. Try to find different ways to do the same thing. You will quickly learn the program. Put down this book right now, go to your computer, and try to create an animation about a bird chasing a bug, a boy walking a dog...anything. As soon as you begin, you will instantly start learning about different ways of telling the same story. The Flash message boards are also a fantastic resource to gain and share knowledge, insights, tips, and tricks, and to show off your latest creations no matter how elementary they may be. Most of all, have fun. Good luck!

Samples

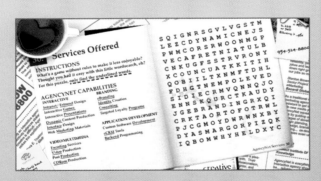

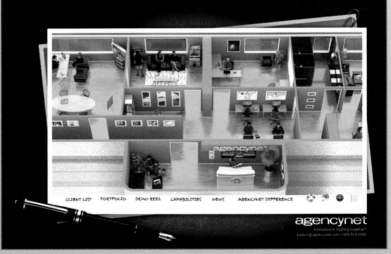

PRO • FILE

Name: Joe Shields

Organization: No. None at all. You should see my desk.

URL: http://www.joecartoon.com

How did you learn Flash? A friend of mine taught me. Brad Yarhouse. We worked together at a children's apparel company as designers. He taught me the basics, and that's all I know. His site is http://www.yarhouse.com. I'm a big fan.

How did you get started using Flash? I used to rent an office downtown. Way back in 1997, a 17-year-old computer geek from down the hall took one of my designs (it was two side-by-side drawings of an alien doing the pelvic thrust) and made a GIF animation out of it. I took one look at it and a big fat light exploded in my head. I was an animator and I didn't even know it. I called up Brad and begged him to teach me.

What feature or tool do you use most often? The Pen tool. I draw a lot of pictures.

What do you like best about Flash? It's easy to use and one guy can make a movie by himself if he wants to.

What sets your animations apart from others? My own personality. It's definitely made, for better or worse, by one guy. I think people can tell. My work has a home-made feel to it—at least, that's what I think. It ain't exactly Disney, now is it?

What is the secret to a great animation? For me, it has to be funny. So I go for what makes me laugh. If you try to make it according to what you think other people will respond to, you're sunk. Stay true to you.

Are there any tips that you can share with the readers about using Flash? I use flash at its most basic level. I draw frame by frame a lot and throw in an occasional button. For me, it's that simple.

Are there any animation tips you can share with our readers? If you have to draw a lot of frames with a similar object—for me, it is mouths—fill one color at a time frame by frame. Then start over with the next color at the beginning. Why? When you have that many frames, its faster to fly from frame to fame with the Fill tool once than it is to select the Fill tool three times, frame by frame. (My mouths are three colors at most—two reds and white.)

Do you have any other advice for teens getting started with Flash animations? Yeah. You have a brain. You have thoughts in there that are yours, and I bet a lot of people could relate to them. So stay true to yourself whether it be funny, sad, serious, whatever. Don't let the bubble poppers tell you that you can't. And when the whole world is barkin' at your door because they love what you did, tell 'em the Joe-man sent you.

Samples

chapter 8
Putting Your Body in Motion

C haracter movement is the cornerstone of almost every animation that you will create. Fortunately, Flash gives you the ability to create this type of movement with relative ease. In the last chapter, you learned that by using keyframes, you can create the illusion that an object is moving when the animation plays by moving the object across the Stage. A more common technique, however, is to make it seem like the character is moving by manipulating the character's joints to mimic the movement of walking or running while moving the background behind the character. Watch almost any cartoon and you'll see this technique at work. When a character runs, he or she doesn't really go anywhere; instead, the character stays in the middle of the screen while the background moves behind him or her. This is exactly what you are going to explore in this chapter. You'll start by creating a very simple "stick man" character made of little lines and a couple of shapes, as well as a background. Then, you'll animate the figure by moving his joints and moving the background behind him.

Creating the Character

The key to creating a character that you want to move in this manner, including the stick man you'll build here, is to build him one part at a time, with each part connected to a key joint. That way, you can animate the various parts to create realistic-looking movement. Here's how it's done:

1. Select the Brush tool.
2. Open the Brush Size drop-down menu and select the fifth option from the top as shown in Figure 8.1.
3. Click the Object Drawing option in the Tools panel if it is not already selected.

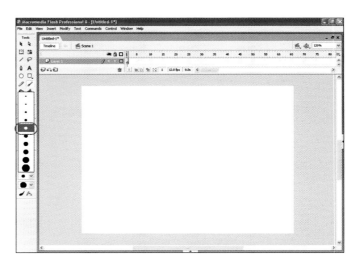

Figure 8.1 Select the fifth size option from the top.

127

4. Draw several lines on the Stage, as shown in Figure 8.2. These lines will make up the arms, legs, and body of your character.

5. Click the Brush Shape drop-down menu and select the oval shape, as shown in Figure 8.3.

6. Click four times on the Stage to create the character's hands and feet.

7. Click the Oval tool, and click and drag on the Stage to create an oval to serve as the character's head, as shown in Figure 8.4.

8. Click the Subselection tool and then click on the edge of the oval. A series of nodes will appear.

9. Click and drag the bottom node to the right to create a chin for your character.

10. Click and drag the middle-left node to the right to create the character's nose. You should now have a side profile of a head, as shown in Figure 8.5.

Animating the Character

To make your character look like it is walking, you'll use the frame-by-frame animation technique that you learned about in the previous chapter. You'll also take advantage of the Onion Skin feature so you can see what is taking place in the frames before and after the selected frame in the animation.

1. Using the Free Transform tool, move and rotate the various parts of the character so that they look like the image you see in Figure 8.6.

2. Click and drag across frames 1–6 to select them.

3. Right-click your selection and select Convert to Keyframes from the menu that appears, as shown in Figure 8.7. The character will now appear on all six frames.

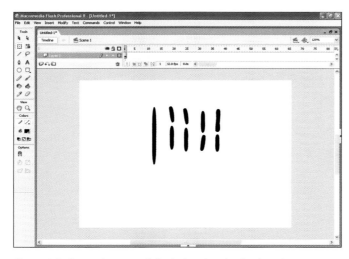

Figure 8.2 Create the parts of the body using the Brush tool.

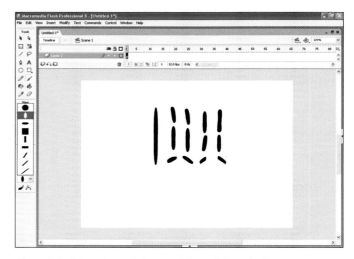

Figure 8.3 Select the oval shape and then click on the Stage to create the hands and feet for your character.

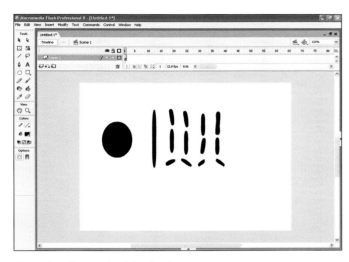

Figure 8.4 Create a head for the character.

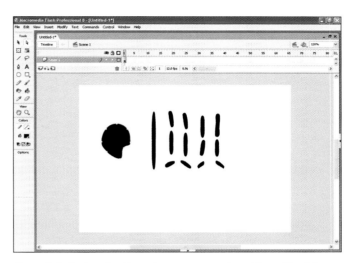

Figure 8.5 By dragging the nodes, you can create a side profile of the head.

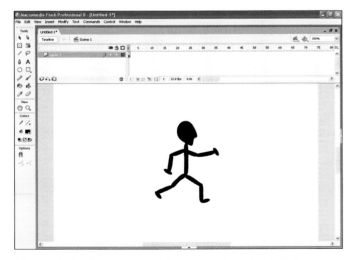

Figure 8.6 Position the parts of character so that it looks like he's walking.

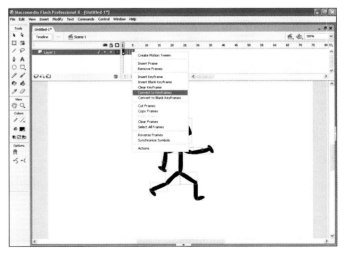

Figure 8.7 Make keyframes out of frames 1–5.

8. Putting Your Body in Motion

4. Click frame 2 to select it.

5. Click the Onion Skin button to turn this feature on.

6. Using the Free Transform tool, move and rotate the parts of the character so that they look like the image you see in Figure 8.8.

7. Click frame 3 and reposition the character's parts as shown in Figure 8.9.

8. Repeat step 6 for the next frame, as shown in Figure 8.10.

9. Click the Onion Skin button to turn this feature off.

10. You now have one complete loop of the character walking; now you need to repeat this animation several times so that it appears as if your character is walking for a while. To do this, you'll simply copy the existing frames and paste them several times. To begin, right-click any frame and choose Select All Frames from the menu that appears.

> A complete segment of an animation (like the character walking that you just created) is called a *motion cycle.*

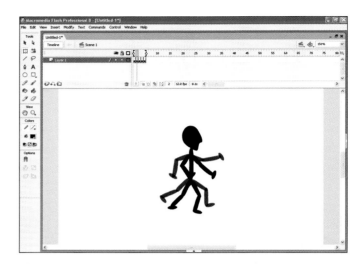

Figure 8.8 Reposition the parts of the character in the second frame so they look like this. Notice that because the Onion Skin feature is turned on, you can see the contents of frame 1 showing through.

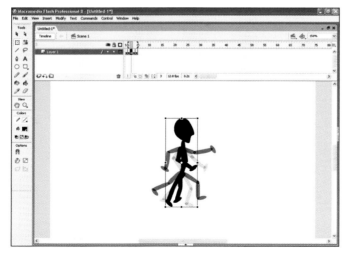

Figure 8.9 Reposition the character in frame 3 as seen here.

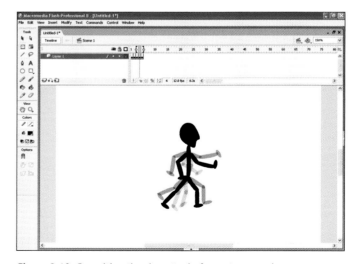

Figure 8.10 Reposition the character in frame 4 as seen here.

11. Press Ctrl+Alt+C to copy the frames.

12. Click the first blank cell in the Timeline, as shown in Figure 8.11. This is where you will paste the frames.

13. Press Ctrl+Alt+V to paste the frames. They will now appear at the end of the first motion cycle.

14. Repeat steps 12 and 13 five more times so that there are a total of 35 frames in your animation, as shown in Figure 8.12.

15. Now that you have 35 frames, it's much easier to make your animation even longer. Go ahead and copy and paste all the existing frames two more times so that you have a considerably longer animation. (Press Ctrl+Alt+A to select all the frames, press Ctrl+Alt+C to copy the selected frames, and then click the first empty frame in the Timeline and press Ctrl+Alt+V. If you played the animation now, your character would walk for about six seconds, which is enough time for you to create a moving background.)

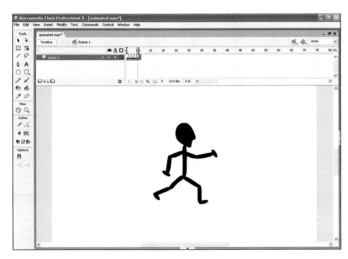

Figure 8.12 By pasting the frames several times, you increase the length of your animation.

Figure 8.11 Select the first empty frame at the end of the animation. This is where you will paste the frames that you copied.

Creating the Background

To create a background that can be animated, you simply draw objects on a separate layer using the tools that you learned about in earlier chapters. The trick here is to create a background that is at least twice as wide as the Stage so that it can be moved during the animation. (This may sound a little confusing, but trust me—it will all make sense in a moment.)

1. Click frame 1 in the Timeline and then click the New Layer button. This creates a brand new layer, layer 2, on which you can draw your background.

2. To keep things organized, rename your two layers. Click the text that reads Layer 2 in the Layers area and type Background to rename it. Then click the text that reads Layer 1 in Layers area type Character to rename it.

3. Currently, your Background layer is on top of your Character layer. Because you want your character to be in front of the background, you need to change the order of the layers. Position your mouse pointer beside the paper icon by the Background layer, click, and drag it downward until a little black line appears under the Character layer, as shown in Figure 8.13.

4. Click the lock icon and the eye icon by the Character layer to lock and hide this layer. That way, there is no chance you will inadvertently make changes to this layer while you are creating the background.

5. Create the background objects as shown in Figure 8.14. The jogging path, grass, and sky are simply rectangles, and the trees and clouds were made using the Brush tool. Notice how none of the clouds or the trees shown here overlap the left or right edge of the background; that's because the animation will restart when it reaches the end. For this reason, the point where the end meets the beginning must be seamless so the person watching won't notice the point where the end meets the beginning. To achieve this, the left edge of your background must look exactly like the right edge.

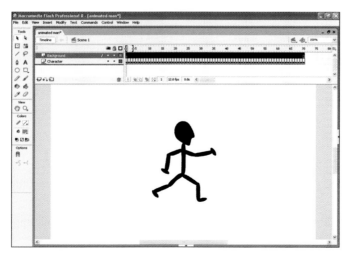

Figure 8.13 Position the Background layer behind the Character layer by dragging downward. Release the mouse button when a little black line appears under the layer, as shown here.

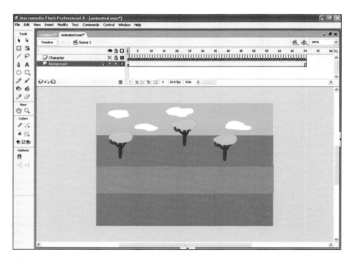

Figure 8.14 Create the background seen here using the Brush and Rectangle tools.

6. After you finish drawing the objects for the background, press Ctrl+A to select them all, and then press Ctrl+C to copy them to the clipboard.

7. Type 45 in the Zoom field in the top-right corner of the screen to change the zoom level to 45 percent, as shown in Figure 8.15. This will allow you to see the entire Stage and more—a necessity because the background you're creating must be at least twice as wide as the Stage.

8. Press Ctrl+V to paste the copy of the background onto the Stage.

9. Press and hold down the right arrow key until the background you pasted is to the right of the original background, but still overlapping it slightly (see Figure 8.16). Make sure you use the right arrow key and not the mouse to move the copy of the background; you need this movement to be very precise.

10. Press Ctrl+A to select all the objects on the Background layer and then press Ctrl+G to group them. Grouping them will make it easier to animate the entire background.

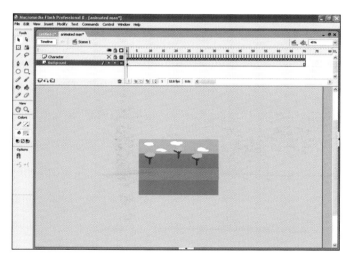

Figure 8.15 Changing the zoom level to 45 percent enables you to see the entire Stage and more.

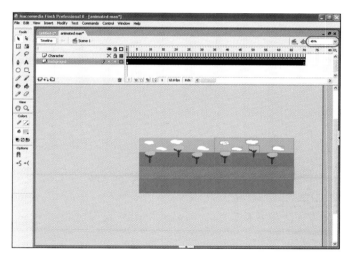

Figure 8.16 Using the right arrow key on the keyboard, move the copy of the background to the right of the original background. Make sure that there is no gap between the two backgrounds. In other words, ensure that they overlap slightly.

8. Putting Your Body in Motion

133

Animating the Background

Now that you've created the background, it's time to animate it. Using a motion tween, you'll move the background from left to right, animating it so that it goes through one motion cycle after it reaches frame 35 (halfway through the animation). You'll then repeat the cycle by copying and pasting the frames.

1. Click frame 35 in the Background layer and press the F6 key on your keyboard. This will create a keyframe.

2. Right-click any frame in the Background layer and select Create Motion Tween from the menu that appears, as shown in Figure 8.17. An arrow should appear in the Timeline starting at the first frame and extending to the keyframe.

3. Click frame 35, and then click the Selection tool.

4. Click once on the background to select it.

5. Press the left arrow key to move the background until its right edge is aligned with the right edge of the Stage, as shown in Figure 8.18.

6. Click the lock and eye icons by the Character layer in the Layers area to unhide and unlock that layer.

7. Click frame 1 in the Character layer and press the Enter or Return key to play your animation. What you should see is the background moving until the playhead reaches frame 35. At that point, the background will simply stop moving.

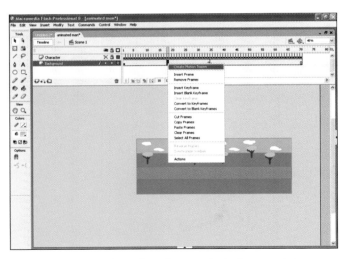

Figure 8.17 Right-click any frame between the keyframes and choose Motion Tween from the menu that appears to create a motion tween.

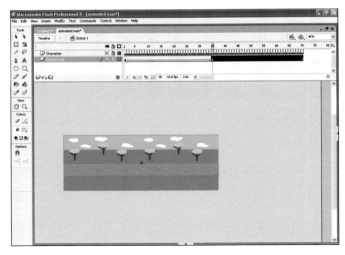

Figure 8.18 Move the background to the right until it is aligned with the right edge of the Stage.

8. To correct this, you need to copy and paste the animation of the background to the last 35 frames. To begin, click and drag across the 35 frames that make up the Background layer. When you release the mouse button they should appear selected, as in Figure 8.19. Now press Ctrl+Alt+C to copy these frames.

9. Click the first empty frame in the Background layer and press Crtl+Alt+V to paste the copied frames into the Timeline. That's it! You've created an animation where the background moves and the character stays in one place.

10. Playing the animation by pressing the Enter or Return key won't give you a true representation of the effect. To really see how the animation looks, press Ctrl+Enter on the keyboard. This will play your animation in a window of its own so you won't see all the extras outside the Stage, as shown in Figure 8.20.

Figure 8.19 Select all the frames in the Background layer.

Figure 8.20 Press Ctrl+Enter to play your animation in its own window.

Now You Try

Try to create an animation that looks similar to the one in Figure 8.21, with the background of stars moving from left to right as the spaceship moves up and down. If you get stuck at any point, follow the steps in this section.

1. Create a spaceship on the default layer that is similar to the one you see in Figure 8.22. Don't worry if it's not exactly the same; just try to create something close. Name the layer Spaceship to help keep things organized.

2. Right-click frame 10 and select Insert Keyframe from the menu that appears. A keyframe will be created on this frame.

Figure 8.21 Create an animation of a spaceship with a background of stars that moves from left to right.

8. Putting Your Body in Motion

135

3. Right-click frame 20 and select Insert Keyframe from the menu that appears. A keyframe will be created on this frame.

4. Right-click frame 9 and select Create Motion Tween. An arrow will appear in the Timeline between frames 1 and 10.

5. Right-click any frame between 10 and 20 and select Create Motion Tween. An arrow will appear in the Timeline between frames 10 and 20, as shown in Figure 8.23.

6. Click frame 10 and move the spaceship up slightly, as shown in Figure 8.24.

7. Press the Enter or Return key. As the animation plays, you should see the spaceship move up and then down again.

8. You need this motion cycle to be repeated several times. To accomplish this, you can copy and paste the frames you just created. To begin, right-click on any frame and choose Select All Frames from the menu that appears. All the frames in the animation will be selected.

9. Right-click anywhere on the selection and choose Copy Frames from the menu that appears.

10. Right-click frame 21 and choose Paste Frames from the menu that appears.

11. Repeat step 10 on frames 41 and 61 (see Figure 8.25).

12. Play your animation. You should see the spaceship go up and down several times.

13. Create a new layer and name it Background.

14. Click and drag the Background layer so that it is under the Spaceship layer in the Layers area.

15. Hide and lock the Spaceship layer by clicking the appropriate icons in the Layers area (see Figure 8.26). This will prevent you from inadvertently selecting or modifying this layer. Make sure that you follow this step, or things won't work in the following steps.

16. Click frame 1 in the Background layer.

17. Select the Rectangle tool and create a black rectangle that is the same size as the Stage.

18. Select the Brush tool and create white dots of different sizes all over the background, as shown in Figure 8.27.

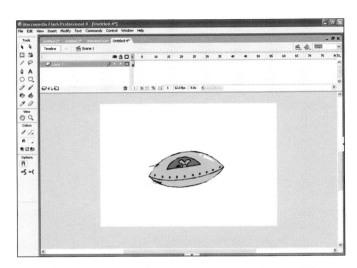

Figure 8.22 Create or import your spaceship onto the Stage and then name the layer that contains it Spaceship.

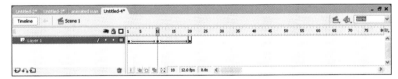

Figure 8.23 Create a motion tween between frames 1 and 10 and 10 and 20.

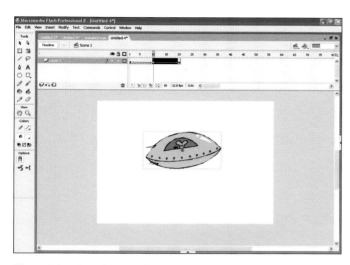

Figure 8.24 Move the spaceship up slightly in the middle keyframe so the spaceship will move up and then down again when the animation is played.

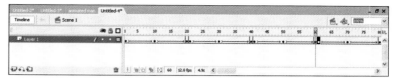

Figure 8.25 Paste the copied selection on frames 21, 41, and 61 to loop the animation several times.

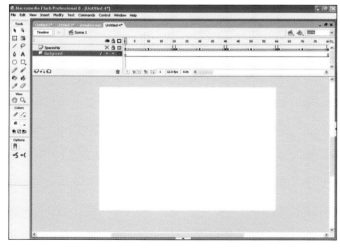

Figure 8.26 Place the Background layer beneath the Spaceship layer, and be sure to hide and lock the Spaceship layer.

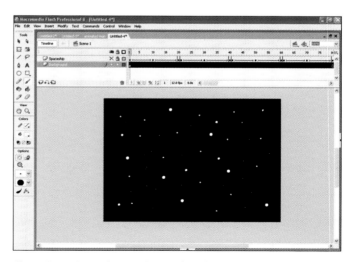

Figure 8.27 Create the stars by painting with different-sized Brush tools.

8. Putting Your Body in Motion

19. Press Ctrl+A to select everything on the layer, and press Ctrl+G to group all the objects on this layer together.

20. Change the zoom level to 65 percent so that you can see the entire rectangle.

21. Press Ctrl+C to copy the background, and press Ctrl+V to paste it onto the Stage.

22. Using the Selection tool, move the copied background to the right of the existing background, making sure it overlaps slightly as shown in Figure 8.28.

23. Press Ctrl+A and then Ctrl+G to group all the objects in the background together.

24. Click frame 20 in the Background layer, and press F6 to create a keyframe.

25. Right-click any frame between frames 1 and 20 and choose Create Motion Tween in the menu that appears. An arrow will appear in the Timeline between frames 1 and 20.

26. Click frame 20 and, using the Selection tool, move the background until the right side of the background is aligned with the right side of the Stage, as shown in Figure 8.29.

27. You created a motion tween, which means that when the animation plays, the background will move from left to right between frames 1 and 20. You now need to copy the background animation several times so that it loops while the animation plays. To begin, click and drag across frames 1–20 in the Background layer to select the frames.

28. Right-click anywhere on the selection and choose Copy Frames in the menu that appears.

29. Right-click frame 21 and select Paste Frames from the menu that appears.

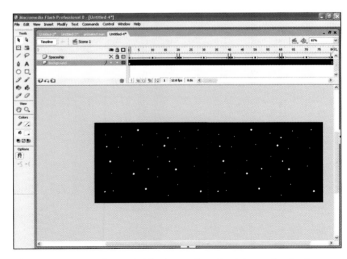

Figure 8.28 Move the copied background to the right, and make it slightly overlap the existing background.

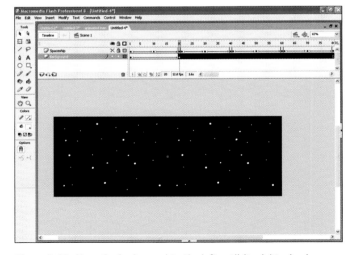

Figure 8.29 Move the background to the left until its right edge is aligned with the right edge of the Stage.

30. Repeat this step on frames 41 and 61 (see Figure 8.30).

31. Press Ctrl+Enter to play the animation in its own window. The spaceship should appear like it's flying.

32. Notice that there are extra frames in the Timeline at the end of the Background layer. This is because when you pasted frames in step 29, it shifted the existing frames to the side. To fix this, begin by clicking and dragging from frame 81 to the end of the animation in the Background layer.

33. Right-click the selection and choose Remove Frames from the menu that appears.

34. Unhide the Spaceship layer and press Ctrl+Enter. The animation should play correctly.

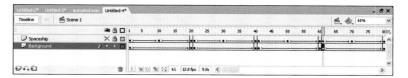

Figure 8.30 Paste the copied frames several times to loop the animation.

chapter 9
Tunes for Your 'Toons

I have an easy assignment for you. I want you to either go out and rent a really good action movie or turn on your favorite television show. Before you start watching, however, turn the volume to zero—then sit back, relax, and enjoy the show.

I'll bet that the experience you have watching your entertainment with no sound wasn't nearly as good as it usually is at the normal volume level. If sound wasn't important to movies, television shows, and video games, then there certainly wouldn't be a category for "best music" on awards nights. In addition to playing a crucial role in movies, on TV, and in video games, sound is essential to great Flash animation.

Sounds and music can add so much to your animations! The most obvious use of sound for your animation would be dialogue for your characters, but that is just one of many examples of how sound can be used. You can create and apply background music, play sounds when certain events happen, or alert the person watching the animation to take a certain action. Music and sounds can help create atmosphere in your animations, changing the mood or enhancing the drama. This chapter explores not only how to apply sounds to your animations, but also how to record and apply dialogue.

Importing Sounds and Music

Say you have a favorite MP3 song that you want to play in the background of your animation. Before you can apply it—or any other sounds—you need to import the music file into your animation. When you import a sound, it is placed in the Library for the animation you are working on and can then be applied to different parts of your animation. Let's begin by going through the process of importing sounds to the Library.

> Most songs have a copyright, which means that if you plan on using them in animation that will be shared on the web or made for sale, you need to get permission from the copyright holder.

1. Start by creating an animation. For this example, I've created a simple animation of a cartoon face with a mouth that moves up and down to make it look as if the character is talking, as shown in Figure 9.1. If you take a look at the Timeline in that image, notice that I created two keyframes within the sequence—a shape tween was applied, and then the mouth shape was changed in each keyframe to create the illusion of movement.

2. Open the File menu, choose Import, and select Import to Library to open the Import to Library dialog box (see Figure 9.2), from which you can select a file to import.

3. Navigate your computer to locate the audio file that you would like to import, select the file, and then click the Open button. The dialog box will disappear and although it will appear as though nothing has changed in your animation, the file you imported will now be available in your Library, and can be applied to your animation.

4. Repeat step 3 for any other audio files you would like to import for your animation.

If you are using Windows, you can import WAV, AIFF, and MP3 files into Flash. If you are using an Apple computer, you can import only MP3 files. If you want to be able to import additional types of audio files to your Mac, download and install the free QuickTime software from Apple's web site (currently http://www.apple.com/quicktime).

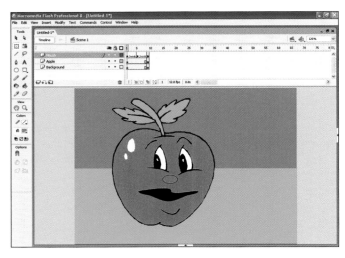

Figure 9.1 Create an animation to which you can later add sound.

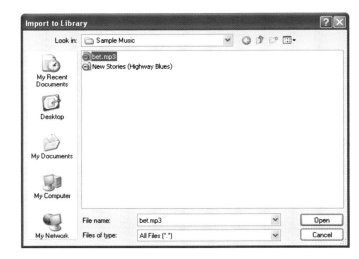

Figure 9.2 Use the Import to Library dialog box to navigate your computer and select audio files for use in your animation.

Inserting Sounds

Once you have imported the audio files you want to use in your animation to the Library, the process of applying them is really quite simple. With just a few clicks of your mouse button you can add the audio. (Note that the audio you add will be inserted on a separate layer.) Here's how it's done:

1. Click the Insert Layer button in the Layers area of the Timeline to create a new layer.
2. Rename the new layer to match the name of the sound you are importing. In this example, I labeled the layer "Sound." By default, this layer will be selected—but make sure it *remains* selected because you will be importing the sound to this layer.
3. Press Ctrl+L to open the Library. If any sounds have been imported prior to now, you'll see a list of them here.
4. Click the sound that you would like to import. A visual representation of the sound (wavy lines) will appear in the top portion of the Library window, as shown in Figure 9.3.
5. If you want to preview the sound file, click the Play button in the top-right corner of the Library window.
6. Click and drag the sound file from the Library to any location on the Stage. When you release the mouse button, you'll notice that the audio has been added to the selected layer, as shown in Figure 9.4.
7. Press the Enter key to play your animation. Notice that the sound starts playing at the beginning of your animation. In the following sections, you'll learn how to change the properties of the sound so that you can choose when and for how long it plays.

> Although you can place more than one sound on a layer, it's a good idea to create a separate layer for each sound that you import.

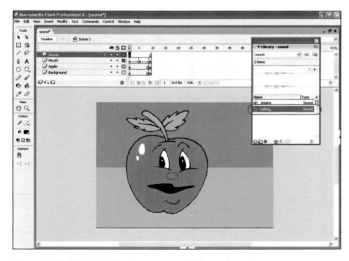

Figure 9.3 Click the file that you would like to import.

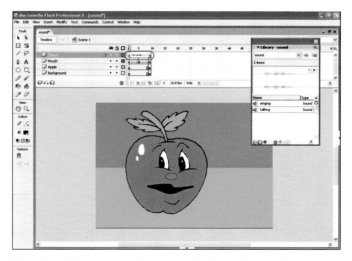

Figure 9.4 After you drag the sound to the Stage, the sound waves appear on the selected layer.

9. Tunes for Your 'Toons

143

Creating Background Music

If you want your song to play over and over while your animation plays, you'll need to make your audio file loop. *Looping* simply means that when your song reaches its end, it will start over again. You can specify how many times you want your audio to loop in the Property inspector.

1. Follow the steps in the sections "Importing Sounds and Music" and "Inserting Sounds" to import a sound and insert it into its own layer.

2. Select the layer that contains the sound that you want to have play over and over in your animation.

3. Click Ctrl+F3 to open the Property inspector. (Alternatively, you can launch the Property inspector by opening the Window menu, choosing Properties, and selecting Properties again.)

4. In the Sync menu, make sure that Event is selected, and choose Loop from the second drop-down list.

5. Rather than having the sound loop over and over, you can specify the number of times you want the sound to repeat. To do so, type a number in the Repeat box (I went with 5).

6. Press the Enter key. Notice in the Timeline in Figure 9.5 that the sound now repeats itself five times and then ends.

TYPES OF SOUNDS

You may have noticed that there are several options in the Sync menu from which you can choose—including the two main types of sounds in Flash:

◆ **Event.** This option, meant for short sounds, is the one you'll probably choose most often in your animations. If your animation will play from a web site, an Event sound won't start playing until the sound has been completely downloaded.

◆ **Stream.** This option will stream your audio, meaning that as soon as part of the sound has been downloaded, the sound will begin to play. This is particularly useful if you have a long song or background music in your animation.

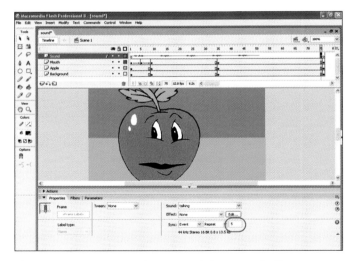

Figure 9.5 You can change the number of times an audio file repeats itself using the Property inspector.

Recording Dialogue

So how, exactly, can you record conversations for your characters? There are dozens of free audio recorders out there that you can use to record your voice and then convert the recording to an audio file that can be used by Flash. In fact, if you are using Windows, you already have a sound recorder—it's built right into your system. To use it to record dialogue, just attach a microphone to your computer and do the following:

1. Click the Start button, choose All Programs, select Accessories, choose Entertainment, and click Sound Recorder.
2. After making sure your microphone is attached to your computer, click the Record button in the Sound Recorder window, as shown in Figure 9.6.
3. Speak the dialogue into the microphone.
4. When you are finished, click the Stop button.
5. Open the File menu and choose Save As.
6. Name the audio file, select the folder where you want it to be saved, and click the Save button. The file will be saved in WAV format and can now be imported into the Library and applied to your animation.

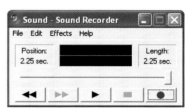

Figure 9.6 Windows Sound Recorder enables you to record audio for use in your animations.

Positioning Audio

You've learned how to place audio in your animation such that it starts at the beginning of the animation. Odds are, though, that you'll want your sound to play at a specific point in the animation—not necessarily at the beginning. This is particularly true when applying sounds like character dialogue, because you want it to synch up with the movement of the character's mouth. Accomplishing this is as simple as creating a keyframe on the frame where you want the sound to start. Here's how:

1. Create an animation and import the necessary sounds to the Library as outlined in the section "Importing Sounds and Music."
2. Create a separate layer for the sound that you want to apply and give that layer an appropriate name.
3. Click the frame where you want the sound to begin playing.
4. Press F6 on your keyboard to create a keyframe on the selected frame. In this example, I wanted my audio file to start playing on frame 10, so I created a keyframe on that frame, as shown in Figure 9.7.
5. If it's not already open, launch the Property inspector by clicking Ctrl+F3. Then, in the Property inspector, open the Sound drop-down list. You'll see a list of all the sounds you have imported; choose the desired sound, as in Figure 9.8.
6. Play your animation. Notice that the sound doesn't start until the keyframe you created. In this example, the sound starts on frame 10, as shown in the Timeline in Figure 9.9.

> These steps also demonstrate an alternate way to apply sounds without having to open the Library.

9. Tunes for Your 'Toons

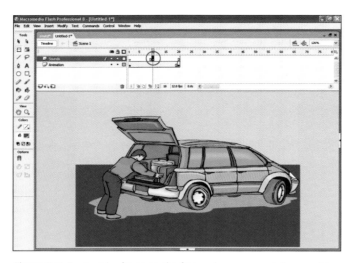

Figure 9.7 Create a keyframe on the frame where you want the sound to begin.

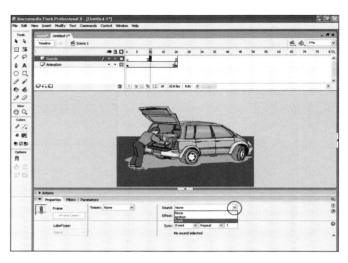

Figure 9.8 Choose the sound you want to apply from the Sound drop-down list.

If you try to insert a sound without creating a keyframe, the sound will be inserted at either the beginning of the animation or on the last keyframe—whichever is closer. For example, say you have a keyframe on frame 10 and one on frame 20. If you try to insert a sound on frame 17, the sound will begin on frame 10, because it is the last keyframe.

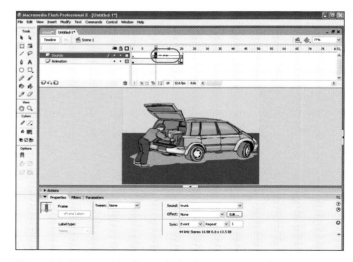

Figure 9.9 The sound begins at the keyframe you created.

Now You Try

Let's take a moment to put to use some of the things you've learned in this chapter by creating an animation with a character who speaks.

1. Create a four-frame animation in which the mouth of the character is closed on frames 1 and 2 and partially open on frames 3 and 4, as shown in Figure 9.10.

2. Copy and paste the four frames several times so that when you play the animation it will seem as though the character is talking because his mouth is opening and closing.

3. Using any sound recorder, such as Window Sound Recorder, record audio of a person saying "Hello, my name is *name*" (where *name* is the name of your choice).

4. Apply the audio you just recorded to your animation.

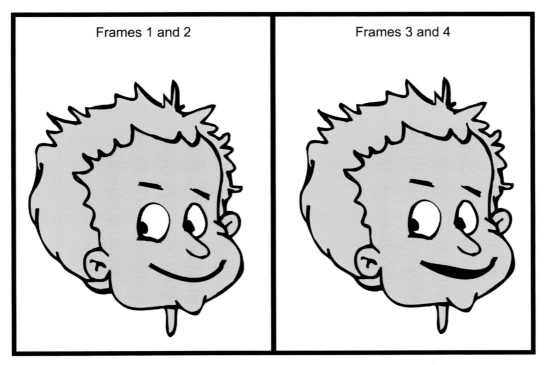

Figure 9.10 Create an animation in which the mouth opens and closes, and then apply some dialogue.

Adding Sound Effects

When I think of sound effects, I always think of the *Star Wars* movies. They had such fantastic sound effects—blasters, aliens, explosions, lightsabers, and so much more. The sound effects available in Flash aren't quite as glamorous as those; they really just give you minor control over how your sounds are played. Fortunately, in addition to allowing you to select from a variety of pre-set effects, you can also create your own. In this section I'll review the presets, while the next section covers the process of creating custom effects.

1. If it's not already open, launch the Property inspector by pressing Ctrl+F3.
2. Click on any frame in the Timeline that contains a sound.
3. Click the Effect drop-down list in the Property inspector and select the desired effect, as shown in Figure 9.11. The list of choices includes the following:

   ◆ **None.** No big surprise here—selecting this option will remove any existing effect you have applied.

   ◆ **Left channel.** Choose this option if you want the sound to play out of the computer's left speaker only.

   ◆ **Right channel.** Choose this option if you want the sound to play out of the computer's right speaker only.

   ◆ **Fade left to right.** When you select this option, the sound will start in the left speaker, and then it will slowly decrease in volume in the left speaker and increase in volume in the right speaker.

   ◆ **Fade right to left.** When you select this option, the sound will start in the right speaker, and then it will decrease in volume in the right speaker and increase in volume in the left speaker.

   ◆ **Fade in.** If you select this option, the volume of the sound will start at zero and then gradually increase to the normal level.

   ◆ **Fade out.** If you select this option, the volume of the sound will start at normal level and then gradually decrease to zero.

   ◆ **Custom.** By choosing this option, you can adjust how quickly a sound fades in and out and from which speaker.

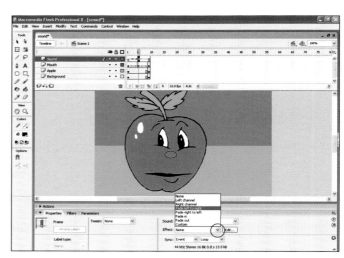

Figure 9.11 Choose any of the sound-effects options from the Effect drop-down list.

Creating Custom Effects

In the last section you learned how to select an effect from a list of pre-sets. In this section you'll learn how to create your own effects.

1. If the Property inspector is not already open, launch it by pressing Ctrl+F3.

2. Click any frame that contains a sound.

3. Click the Edit button in the Property inspector to open the Edit Envelope dialog box. The top pane in the Edit Envelope dialog box controls the left channel (that is, the music that will come out of the left speaker) and the bottom pane controls the right channel.

4. Position the mouse pointer over the white box in the top-left corner of the top pane, click, and drag downward to adjust the volume level of the left channel, as shown in Figure 9.12.

5. Repeat step 4 in the bottom pane to adjust the volume level for the right channel.

6. If you wish, you can control the volume of the sound in both the left and right channel at different points in the file. To do so, position the mouse pointer anywhere over the volume line in either pane of the Edit Envelope dialog box, click, and drag upward or downward to increase or decrease the volume at that specific point. Repeat this step at different points, as shown in Figure 9.13, and then click OK.

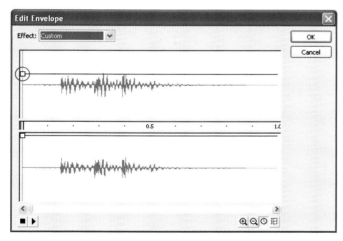

Figure 9.12 Click and drag the white box up or down to adjust the volume level for the left channel.

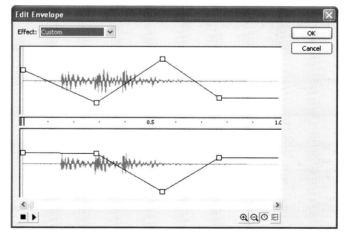

Figure 9.13 Click and drag upward or downward at different points on the line to increase or decrease the volume.

9. Tunes for Your 'Toons

149

Configuring Buttons for Sound

If you're looking to make your Flash animations interactive, buttons are one way to go. Among other things, you can assign sounds to a button so that whenever it is clicked, that sound will play. In this section you'll learn how to do exactly that—create a button and then apply a sound to it.

To make a button, begin by creating the object that you want to act as a button and then convert that object into a symbol, which is an object that you can use over and over again. Here's how:

1. Create the object you want to use as a button and then select it.

2. With the object selected, press the F8 key to launch the Convert to Symbol dialog box.

3. In the Name field, type a name for the button. This can be any name you want.

4. Click the Button option button, as shown in Figure 9.14, and then click OK. You have now created a button to which you can apply a sound.

5. Press Ctrl+L to open the Library, which is the storage location for the symbols you create. You should see the button you just created listed in the Library window.

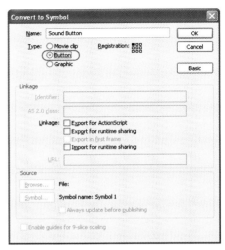

Figure 9.14 Select the Button option button and click OK.

After you create your button object, it's time to apply a sound to it. Any sound you've imported into Flash can be used; if you haven't yet imported the sound you want to use, take a moment to do so now (refer to the section "Importing Sounds and Music" earlier in this chapter for guidance). Then, do the following:

1. Right-click the name of your button in the Library window and choose Edit from the menu that appears, as shown in Figure 9.15.

2. Take a look at the Timeline and notice the four words at the top: Up, Over, Down, and Hit. Each word describes a button's state:

   ◆ **Up.** This is the state of your button if it has not been clicked and the mouse pointer is not currently hovering over it.

   ◆ **Over.** This is the state of your button when the mouse pointer hovers over it.

   ◆ **Down.** This is the state of your button when it has been clicked.

   ◆ **Hit.** This state lets you define the area around your button. The Hit frame is not visible on the Stage on playback, but it defines the area of the button when clicked.

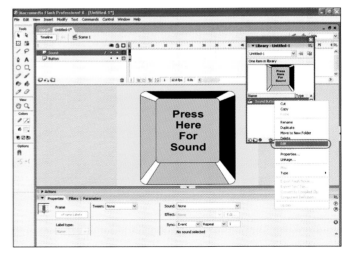

Figure 9.15 Right-click the button name and select Edit from the menu that appears.

Every button you create has these four states, and you can change the attributes of the button for each state—say, making it so that the color of the button changes when it's in the over state or, as in our case, making it so that a sound is played when the button is clicked (that is, when the button is in the down state). To begin, right-click the frame below the down state in the Timeline and select Insert Keyframe from the menu that appears, as shown in Figure 9.16. A dot will appear in the frame, indicating that a keyframe has been created.

3. If the Property inspector is not already open, launch it by pressing Ctrl+F3.

4. Open the Sound drop-down list in the Property inspector and select the desired sound, as shown in Figure 9.17. The sound is applied to the button's down state; when the button is clicked, the sound will play.

5. Click the Scene 1 link at the top of the Timeline to return to regular editing mode (see Figure 9.18).

6. Press Ctrl+Enter to preview the Flash movie.

7. Click the button you created to hear the sound play.

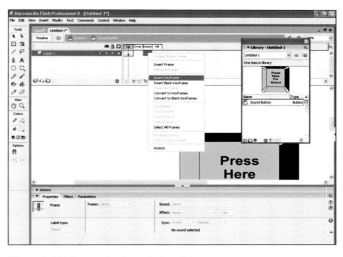

Figure 9.16 Create a keyframe below the down state.

Figure 9.17 Choose a sound from the drop-down list.

Figure 9.18 Click the Scene 1 link to exit the button-editing mode.

Compressing Your Sound

One of the drawbacks of using sound in your Flash animations is that some sound files can be extremely large, especially MP3 sound files. This isn't a problem if you're just watching your animation on your own computer, but if you plan to send your animations to others or post them on a web site, you'll need to reduce the size of the sound files. This can be done during the export process. Here's how it works:

1. Open the File menu, choose Export, and select Export Movie to launch the Export Movie dialog box.

2. Type a name for your movie in the File Name field.

3. Open the Save as Type drop-down list and choose Flash Movie (*.swf), as shown in Figure 9.19. (SWF is the default file format for export, and SWF files can be viewed on most computers that have the Flash plug-in for their Internet browsers.)

4. Click the Save button.

5. In the Export Flash Player dialog box, shown in Figure 9.20, click the Set button next to either Audio Event or Audio Stream. (The option you choose depends on whether your animation contains streaming audio, audio events, or both. If your animation contains both types of audio, you'll need to repeat this step and the next one for each type.)

Figure 9.19 You can choose from a variety of formats when exporting your files.

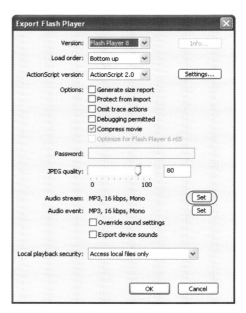

Figure 9.20 Click the Set button(s) in this dialog box to change the audio settings.

6. In the Sound Settings dialog box that opens, open the Compression drop-down list and select one of the available choices, as shown in Figure 9.21. Your choices include the following:

◆ **ADPCM.** Choose this option if you have short audio events in your animation. It only works for 8-bit or 16-bit audio files.

◆ **MP3.** This compression method is meant for use on longer audio files.

◆ **RAW.** Your audio files will not be compressed if this option is selected.

◆ **Speech.** This compression method is best suited for animations with a lot of dialogue.

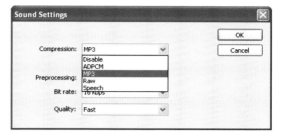

Figure 9.21 Choose from any of the compression options.

7. Depending on the option you select in step 6, you may be presented with several Bit Rate and Sample Rate options. Generally speaking, the lower the rate you select, the smaller the file size—but the poorer the sound quality. Choose a rate for your audio and click OK.

8. Click OK in the Export Flash Player dialog box to export your movie.

chapter 10
Cool Flash Effects

H aving the ability to swing a golf club does not make you Tiger Woods. Just because you can sink a few baskets at your school gym doesn't mean that screaming fans will be seeking your autograph any time soon. And scoring a touchdown in a pick-up flag football game won't guarantee that you'll make it into the NFL Hall of Fame. The point I'm trying to make is that understanding the basics of something doesn't make you a pro.

The same holds true with Flash. Just about anybody can learn the basics of creating animations, just as you have in this book. What separates the pros from the amateurs is practice, and the pros' ability to combine and apply their basic knowledge to create some outstanding effects. This chapter is designed to give you a jump start on creating your own unique effects by showing you how to create some of the more popular cool and unusual Flash effects. Some are relatively simple, while others require quite a few steps. Once you get the hang of creating these effects, you'll be equipped to create animations with your own distinctive style!

Ghost Typing

Unless you've seen it in reruns, you're probably too young to remember the TV show "Doogie Howser M.D." The show chronicled the adventures of a boy genius, played by Neil Patrick Harris, who, by age 16, had become a doctor. At the end of every show, Doogie summarized the lessons he learned by typing an entry into his computer diary; as he typed, viewers watched the text appear on the screen.

Having text appear on the screen as if it was being typed by a ghost is a great effect that can be re-created in your Flash animations. In fact, the effect is relatively easy to create. Here's how it's done:

1. Start by creating a new Flash document.

2. Select the Text tool and click the spot on the Stage where you would like your text to begin.

3. To establish the attributes of the text, including the font, size, and color, press Ctrl+F3 to launch the Property inspector and adjust the settings as needed.

4. Type the complete phrase that you want to appear onscreen after all the text has been "typed" in your animation. For this example, I've typed the phrase Ghost typing is cool with an underscore (_) at the end, as shown in Figure 10.1. (This underscore will act as the cursor in your animation.)

5. Click and drag across frames 1–50 in the Timeline to select them.

6. Right-click any of the selected frames and choose Convert to Keyframes from the menu that appears, as shown in Figure 10.2. All the selected frames will now be keyframes, and will contain the phrase that you typed in step 4.

7. Click frame 1 in the Timeline to select it.

8. Using the Text tool, click and drag across your phrase, starting at the second letter and ending at the last letter, as shown in Figure 10.3. Do not include the underscore in your selection.

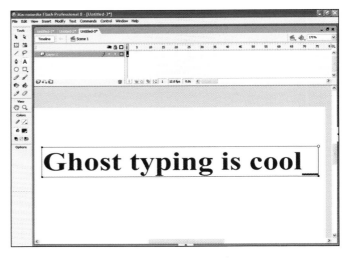

Figure 10.1 Include an underscore at the end of your text.

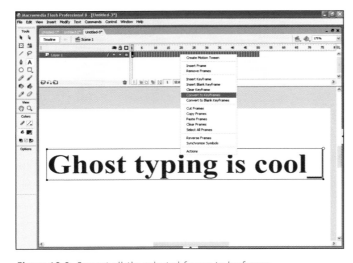

Figure 10.2 Convert all the selected frames to keyframes.

Figure 10.3 Select all the text except the first letter and the underscore.

9. Press the Delete key on your keyboard. You should be left with just the first letter and the underscore, as shown in Figure 10.4.

10. Click frame 2 and, using the Text tool, delete all the letters except for the first and second letters and the underscore.

11. Repeat step 10 on the subsequent frames until the entire phrase appears. Here's how the frames should look:

    Frame 1: G_
    Frame 2: Gh_
    Frame 3: Gho_
    Frame 4: Ghos_
    Frame 5: Ghost_
    Frame 6: Ghost _ (notice the space after the word Ghost)
    Frame 7: Ghost t_

    and so on until frame 21, where the full phrase will appear.

12. Press Enter to play your animation. The letters should magically appear onscreen, as if being typed by a ghost at your keyboard.

> The number of frames it takes for your full phrase to appear will depend on the number of words and letters in your phrase. In this example, it takes 21 frames because there are 18 letters, two spaces in between the words, and one underscore after the words for a total of 21 frames.

Figure 10.4 Delete the selection so that all that remains are the first letter and the underscore.

Now You Try

The animation you just created should contain plenty of leftover keyframes, because you used only 21 frames but created 50. Let's use the remaining keyframes, which occur after the phrase has been typed, to flash the cursor for 10 frames, delete the word "cool" letter by letter, and then replace it with the word "neat." Try this on your own; if you get stuck, follow these steps:

1. Click frame 22 to select it.

2. Using the Text tool, highlight the underscore, and then press the Delete key to remove it, as shown in Figure 10.5.

3. Repeat step 2 on frames 24, 26, 28, and 30 to create the illusion of a flashing cursor when the animation is played.

4. Click frame 31 to select it.

5. Using the Text tool, select and delete the letter "l" at the end of "cool," as shown in Figure 10.6. (Be sure to select only the letter "l" and not the underscore.)

6. Repeat step 5 on frames 32–34, removing one more letter in the word "cool" in each frame. The frames should look like this:

Frame 31: Ghost typing is coo_

Frame 32: Ghost typing is co_

Frame 33: Ghost typing is c_

Frame 34: Ghost typing is _

7. Click frame 35 to select it.

8. Using the Text tool, replace the word "cool" with the letter "n," as shown in Figure 10.7.

9. In frames 36–38, replace the word "cool" with the remaining letters of the word "neat," as shown in Figure 10.8.

10. Your animation is complete, but you still have 12 extra frames at the end. To remove them, click and drag across frames 39–50 in the Timeline to select them, right-click anywhere on the selection, and choose Remove Frames from the menu that appears.

11. Press the Enter key to preview your animation.

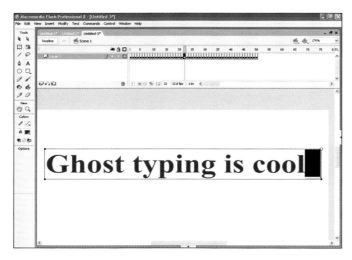

Figure 10.5 Highlight and then delete the underscore in every second frame in frames 22–30 to create the illusion of a flashing cursor.

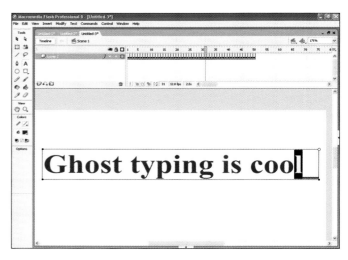

Figure 10.6 Remove the "l" in "cool" but keep the underscore.

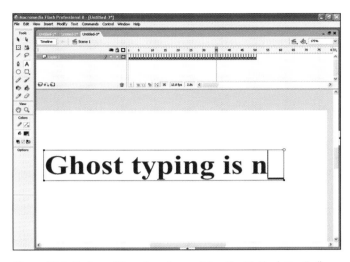

Figure 10.7 In frame 35, replace the word "cool" with the letter "n."

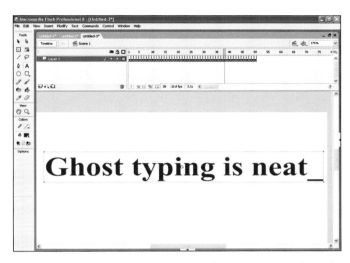

Figure 10.8 Add a letter to each successive frame until the word "neat" is fully spelled.

Fading In and Out

You know how in *Star Trek*, when characters beamed themselves out of the Enterprise, they would step into the transporter and their bodies would fade out, and then fade back in at the new location? You can create the same effect with objects in your animations. To learn how, let's create an alien that will fade out on one side of the Stage and then fade in on the other side. This alien will be made up of many different parts, which means you have two options. One is to put each part on a separate layer and then have each part fade out and in to create a "perfect" fade in and out. The other is to fade all the parts together, which won't look as smooth but will create a cool effect in which part of the alien will fly in. This example goes the "cool" route. I started by creating an alien background scene on its own layer and creating a keyframe on frame 20 of that layer so that the background would appear on all 20 frames. Then I did the following:

1. Create a character or import one to fade in and out on its own layer, as shown in Figure 10.9. Be sure to give the character's layer a descriptive name; I chose "Alien."

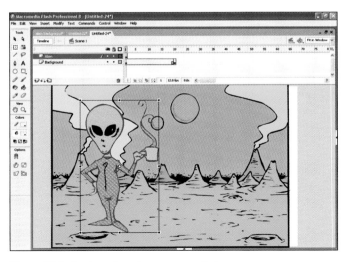

Figure 10.9 Create a character on a separate layer.

2. With your character selected, right-click frame 10 in the Alien layer and select Insert Keyframe from the menu that appears. The alien will now appear on the first 10 frames.

3. Click frame 1 in the Alien layer to select the frame.

4. If the Property inspector is not already open, press Ctrl+F3 to launch it.

5. In the Tween drop-down list, choose Shape, as shown in Figure 10.10.

> The Shape Tween option will not work with any grouped objects.

6. Click frame 10 in the Alien layer to select it.

7. Press Shift+F9 to open the Color Mixer on the right side of the screen.

8. Type 0 in the Alpha field and press Enter. Depending on the makeup of your character, you might still see a solid fill of it (see Figure 10.11), or it may be completely gone. Either way, when you play your animation, the character will completely disappear by the time the animation reaches frame 10.

9. Press Shift+F9 to close the Color Mixer.

10. Click frame 1 and then press the Enter key to run your animation. Depending on how many objects make up your character, the character may fade evenly or certain parts may fly off as they fade. Either way, the desired effect has been achieved.

11. Now it's time to make your character fade back in. To do so, simply copy the existing frames and then reverse them. Begin by clicking and dragging across frames 1–10 in the Alien layer to select them.

12. Right-click anywhere on the selection and choose Copy Frames from the menu that appears, as shown in Figure 10.12.

13. Right-click frame 11 and select Paste Frames from the menu that appears.

14. Click and drag across frames 11–20 in the Alien layer to select the frames you just pasted.

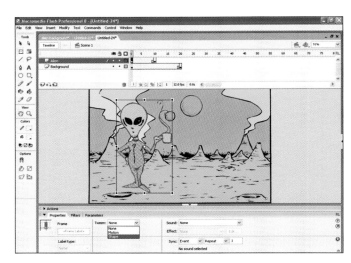

Figure 10.10 Apply a shape tween to your character.

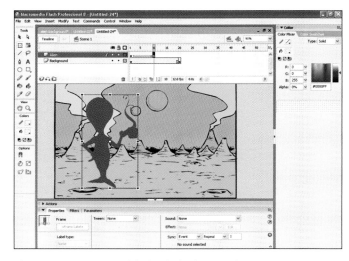

Figure 10.11 Enter an Alpha level of 0 for your character.

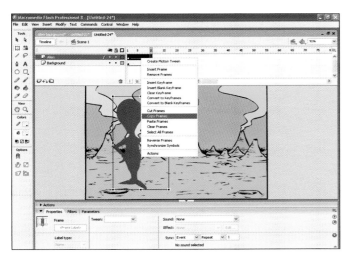

Figure 10.12 Copy the selected frames.

Figure 10.13 Select Reverse Frames from the menu that appears.

15. Right-click your selection and choose Reverse Frames from the menu that appears, as shown in Figure 10.13. This will reverse the order of the frames that you pasted; rather than fading out, they will now fade in.

16. Play the animation; you should see your character fade out and then fade back in—but not at a different location on the screen as planned. To make it so that the alien fades out on the left side of the screen and then fades back in on the right, you'll need to complete a few more steps.

17. Click frame 11 in the Alien layer to select that frame.

18. Using the Selection tool, move the character to the right side of the Stage.

19. You now need to move the character in frame 20 to the exact same position as in frame 11. To do so, you can use the Onion Skin feature. Begin by clicking frame 20 in the Alien layer to select that frame.

20. Click the Onion Skin Outline button in the Timeline.

21. Click and drag the Start Onion Skin marker to frame 11 in the Timeline. You should see a series of outlines in your animation, as shown in Figure 10.14.

Figure 10.14 Turn on the Onion Skin Outlines feature and move the Start Onion Skin marker to frame 11.

22. Using the Selection tool, position the character in frame 20 so that it perfectly matches the right-most Onion Skin outline, as shown in Figure 10.15.

23. Turn off the Onion Skin feature and then play your animation. You should see your character fade out (depending on its makeup, certain parts may fly out as they fade) and then fade or fly in on the other side of your screen.

Now You Try

In the animation you just created, your alien faded out and then instantly faded back in. Try to re-create the animation, this time adding a few-seconds pause between the moment the alien fades out to the moment when it starts to fade in. If you get stuck, follow these steps:

1. Click frame 10 to select it. This frame is the frame in which the alien has completely faded out when the animation is played.

2. Press F5 five times to insert five frames. This creates a slight pause before the animation fades back in.

Applying an Extreme Close-Up

The extreme close-up, which creates the illusion that you are zooming into a specific object on the Stage, takes only a few seconds to create but can have a very powerful result. Here's how it works:

> Until now, you've used vector objects that you have either created or imported into your animation. For this effect, a photograph will be used—although you can re-create the effect with any type of object.

1. Create a new Flash document.

2. Press Ctrl+R to launch the Import dialog box, shown in Figure 10.16.

3. Locate and select the photo that you would like to use for this effect. (I've selected an image included in Windows' Sample Pictures folder; if you are using Windows XP, you should also have access to the same images.)

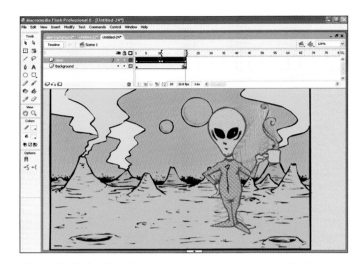

Figure 10.15 Position the character so that it matches up with the right-most outline.

Figure 10.16 Select a photo to import to the Stage.

4. Click the Open button. The photo will be imported and resized to fit the Stage perfectly.

5. Right-click frame 20 and choose Insert Keyframe from the menu that appears. You now have a 20-frame animation of the photo.

6. Right-click any frame between 1 and 19 and choose Create Motion Tween from the menu that appears. There should now be an arrow in the Timeline between frames 1 and 20.

7. Click frame 20 to select it.

8. Select 25% from the Zoom drop-down list located in the top-right corner of the screen, as shown in Figure 10.17.

9. Using the Free Transform tool, position the mouse pointer over any of the corner handles surrounding the image. Then, holding down the Shift key to constrain the motion, click and drag outward. Release the mouse button when the preview of the photo takes up most of the screen, as shown in Figure 10.18.

10. Press Ctrl+Enter to see a preview of the animation. It should appear as if you are zooming into the picture.

Seems like magic, huh? The truth is, this works because when your animation plays, the viewer can see only what takes place on the Stage—and when you enlarged the photo, the outer portions of it spilled *off* the Stage and became invisible to the viewer. The motion tween then made it appear as though a camera was zooming in on the middle of the photo.

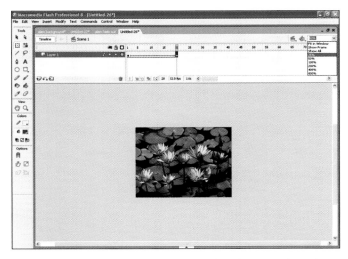

Figure 10.17 Change the zoom level to 25% in order to see the entire Stage and more.

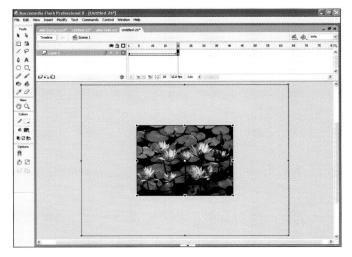

Figure 10.18 As you drag outward, a preview of the new size of the photo appears. Release the mouse button when the preview is as large as the one seen here.

10. Cool Flash Effects

163

Masking

So far, I haven't talked about masking, but I think you're ready to learn about this very, *very* cool feature, which allows you to create some very interesting effects. When a mask is applied to a layer, it, well, *masks* the layer that is underneath it, making that layer invisible. Any object you place on a mask will become a hole in the mask through which the part of the invisible layer underneath the hole will be revealed. Sound confusing? Don't worry. Before I get into any fancy masking effects, I'll show you how to create and apply a simple mask so that you can get a solid understanding of how it works. I promise that once you master it, you'll use masking over and over!

> As in the previous section, a photograph will be used to demonstrate this effect—although you can re-create the effect with any type of object.

1. Create a new Flash document.

2. Press Ctrl+R to launch the Import dialog box.

3. Locate and select any photo. As in the previous section, I've selected one that's included in Windows' Sample Pictures folder.

4. Click the Open button. The photo will be imported and resized to fit the Stage perfectly. (If for any reason your image isn't resized to fit the Stage perfectly, resize it yourself using the Free Transform tool.)

5. Rename the layer that contains your photo "Photo," as shown in Figure 10.19, to help you keep track of things.

6. Click the Insert Layer button to create a new layer, and name this layer "Our Mask." You'll use this layer to mask the Photo layer beneath it.

7. Create a circle with a fill on the Our Mask layer, as shown in Figure 10.20. This circle will act as the hole in the mask, revealing a portion of the Photo layer beneath it.

8. Right-click the Our Mask layer in the Layers section of the Timeline and choose Mask from the menu that appears, as shown in Figure 10.21. The Photo layer will now be invisible, except where the "hole" you created is located.

Figure 10.19 Rename the layer "Photo."

9. Notice in the Layers palette of the Timeline how, once a mask is applied, the icons beside the Our Mask and Photo layers have changed to indicate that a mask has been applied. Also notice that both the layers are locked—that's required in order for the mask effect to work. If you want to modify any of the objects on the Stage, you must first unlock the layers; to do so, click the lock icon next to the Our Mask layer in the Layers palette.

10. You should again see the circle and the photo. Using the Selection tool, move the circle to a new location on the Stage, as shown in Figure 10.22.

11. Click the lock icon to re-lock the layer. Notice that the "hole" has been moved, revealing a new portion of the Photo layer as shown in Figure 10.23.

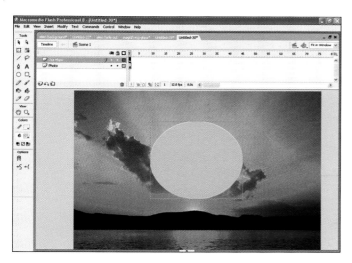

Figure 10.20 Create a circle with a fill on the Our Mask layer.

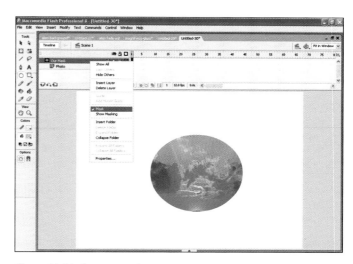

Figure 10.21 Create a mask.

Figure 10.22 Move the circle to a new location.

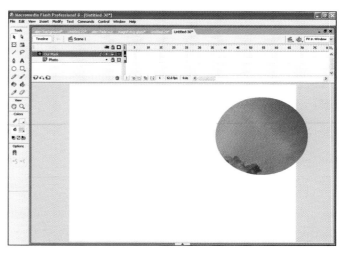

Figure 10.23 By moving the circle, you change what portion of the Photo layer is visible.

10. Cool Flash Effects

Okay, you're probably wondering how this effect can be made a bit more exciting. Well, by animating the objects you create as the holes, changing the shapes of the holes, and changing the layers, you can create a variety of different effects using masks. You'll explore some of these effects in the sections that follow.

Creating a Magnifying Glass Effect

By manipulating the mask technique covered in the last section, you can create the illusion of a magnifying glass moving over an object. The object over which you choose to move can be one that you create in Flash or another vector image or photo that you import. In the following example, I used a map.

1. Create an object on the Stage and name the layer containing the object "Normal Size."

2. With the object selected, press Ctrl+C to copy it.

3. Create a new layer and name it "Magnified."

4. Click the drop-down list in the top-right corner of the screen and choose 50% to change the zoom level, as shown in Figure 10.24.

5. Press Ctrl+V to paste the object onto the Magnified layer.

6. Select the Free Transform tool and position the mouse pointer over one of the object's corner handles. Then, while holding down the Shift key, click and drag outward until the object is almost twice as large as its original size, as shown in Figure 10.25.

7. Create a new layer and call it "Magnifying Glass."

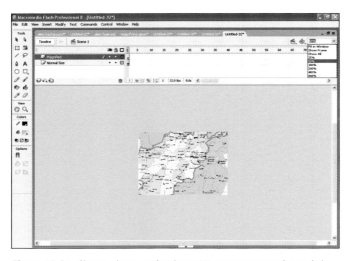

Figure 10.24 Change the zoom level to 50% so you can see beyond the Stage.

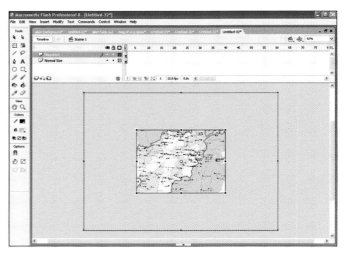

Figure 10.25 The object on the Magnified layer should be almost twice as large as the original.

8. Change the zoom level back to 100% so you can see things in perspective.

9. Create a circle on the Magnifying Glass layer with a black outline and any color fill, as shown in Figure 10.26. This circle will act as your magnifying glass after the mask is created.

10. Right-click the Magnifying Glass layer and select Mask from the menu that appears to see a preview of how the magnifying glass will work. The area where you created your circle will seem magnified, as shown in Figure 10.27.

11. So far you've created a layer mask that looks like a magnifying glass, but you don't have any animation. In the next few steps you'll animate the glass so that it moves around and magnifies different areas of the map. To begin, right-click frame 10 in the Normal Size layer and select Insert Keyframe from the menu that appears.

12. Repeat step 11 on the Magnified layer and on the Magnifying Glass layer. At this point, you should have three keyframes on frame 10, as shown in Figure 10.28.

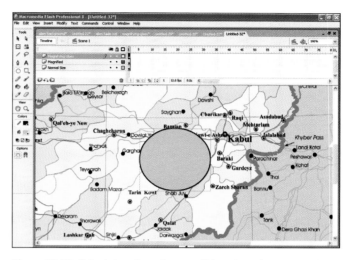

Figure 10.26 This circle acts as the magnifying glass when you create the layer mask.

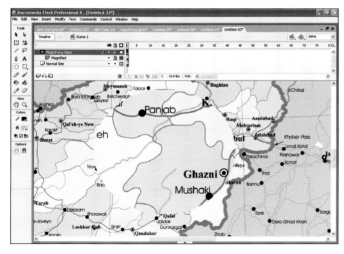

Figure 10.27 The area where you created the circle appears magnified.

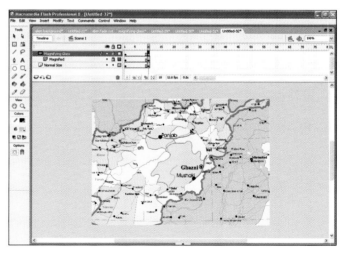

Figure 10.28 Create keyframes on frame 10 of each layer.

10. Cool Flash Effects

13. Right-click any frame in the Magnifying Glass layer between frames 1 and 9 and choose Create Motion Tween from the menu that appears to apply a motion tween to this layer.

14. To actually edit the motion tween, you'll need to unlock the layer. To begin, click frame 10 to select it.

15. Click the lock icon in the Magnifying Glass layer to unlock the layer. You'll now see the magnifying glass circle and the enlarged map again.

16. Using the Selection tool, move the circle to another location on the Stage, as shown in Figure 10.29.

17. Click the lock icon again to re-lock the layer.

18. Press the Enter key to play the animation. As the animation plays, the magnifying glass will move and the spot of magnification will change accordingly, as shown in Figure 10.30.

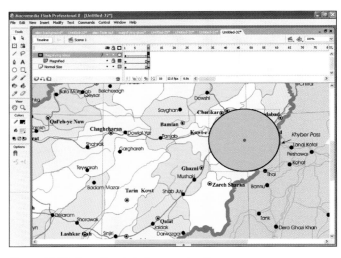

Figure 10.29 Move the circle to a new location.

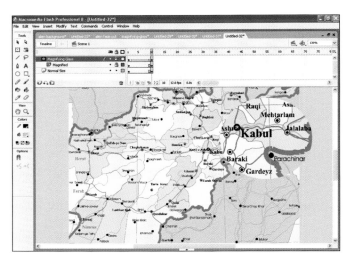

Figure 10.30 As the circle moves, so too does the area of magnification.

Changing the Color Bar

At this point, you should realize that all you need to do when masking is create two versions of an image and then decide where you want to create and animate holes in the mask. In the last example, the holes revealed magnified areas of the image; in this one, rather than making one version of a photo bigger than the other to create a zoom effect, you'll change the color of the photo so that when the hole passes over it, the image will change colors. Of course, Flash isn't a photo editor, so you'll have to use another program to change the color of your image. If you're using Windows, you can use the Paint program included with the operating system, as outlined in the first five steps that follow. If you use an Apple, use any photo editor to slightly change the color of an image, and then begin at step 9.

1. Click the Start button, choose All Programs, select Accessories, and choose Paint to launch the Paint program that comes with the Windows OS.

2. Open the File menu and choose Open to launch the Open dialog box, from which you can select a photo. In this example, I've chosen Blue Hills, which is an image that comes with Windows, but you can select any photo that you like.

3. With the desired image selected, click the Open button.

4. Press Ctrl+I to invert the color of the image, as shown in Figure 10.31. (If you're not using Windows, or if you're more comfortable using other graphics applications, alter the photo in any way you like.)

5. Open the File menu and choose Save As.

6. In the Save As dialog box, save the image with a new name (I added the numeral "1" to the filename, making it Blue Hills1).

7. Click the Save button.

8. Close the Paint program and return to Flash.

9. In Flash, press Ctrl+R to open the Import dialog box.

10. Select the original image—in this case, Blue Hills—and click Open. The image will be imported to the Stage as shown in Figure 10.32.

11. Name the layer with the image you just imported "Original."

12. Click the Insert Layer button in the Layers palette to create a new layer.

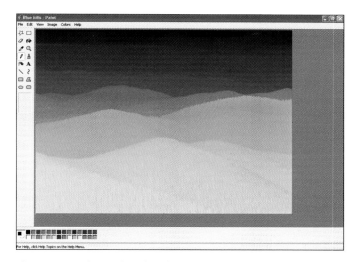

Figure 10.31 Change the color of the image.

Figure 10.32 Import the original image to the Stage.

10. Cool Flash Effects

169

13. Call the new layer "Colored."

14. Press Ctrl+R to open the Import dialog box.

15. Click the file you created in steps 5–7 (in this case, Blue Hills1) and click the Open button. The file will be imported to the Stage, as shown in Figure 10.33.

16. Click the Insert Layer button in the Layers palette to create a new layer, and call this new layer "Mask."

17. Create a rectangle that spans the height of the picture and is similar in width to the one shown in Figure 10.34. This rectangle will act as the "hole" when you create the mask.

18. Right-click the Mask layer and choose Mask from the menu that appears.

19. Now it's time to animate your objects. To begin, right-click frame 10 in the Original layer and select Insert Keyframe from the menu that appears.

20. Repeat step 19 on the Colored layer and on the Mask layer. At this point, you should have three keyframes on frame 10, as shown in Figure 10.35.

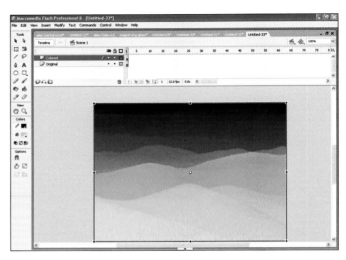

Figure 10.33 Import the manipulated photo to its own separate layer.

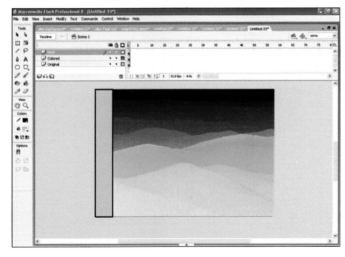

Figure 10.34 Create a rectangle the same height as the picture and the same width as the one seen here.

Figure 10.35 Create keyframes on frame 10 of each layer.

21. Right-click any frame between frames 1 and 9 of the Mask layer and choose Create Motion Tween from the menu that appears to apply a motion tween on this layer.

22. In order to edit the motion tween, you'll need to unlock the Mask layer. To begin, click frame 10 to select it.

23. Click the lock icon in the Mask layer to unlock the layer. You'll now see the rectangle with the fill color over the color-altered photo. Using the Selection tool, move the rectangle to the opposite side of the Stage, as shown in Figure 10.36.

24. Click the lock icon again to re-lock the layer.

25. Press Ctrl+Enter to play the animation. As the animation plays, the rectangle will move across the Stage. As it does, you'll see the altered-color image in the rectangle, as shown in Figure 10.37.

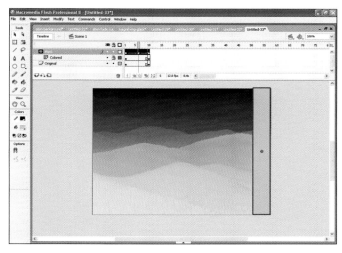

Figure 10.36 Position the rectangle on the far-right side of the Stage.

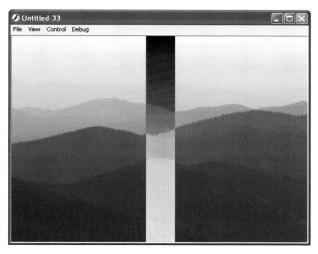

Figure 10.37 When you play the animation, the bar will move and you'll see the altered image in the bar.

10. Cool Flash Effects

171

Creating Dancing Cartoon Lines

The last of the mask effects I'll cover is one that creates the illusion of electricity or movement, which I call "dancing cartoon lines." The end result of the effect is that lines will seemingly move around one of your objects. You've probably seen this type of effect in other animations, cartoons, and commercials; it's a great way to bring focus to a particular object.

1. Create or import an image on the Stage. In this example, I've used a photograph of a car.

2. Call the layer that contains your image "Original."

3. Create a new layer by clicking the Insert Layer button in the Layers palette.

4. Call the new layer "Lines."

5. Using the Pen tool, click various locations around the car in the Lines layer to create an outline around it, as shown in Figure 10.38.

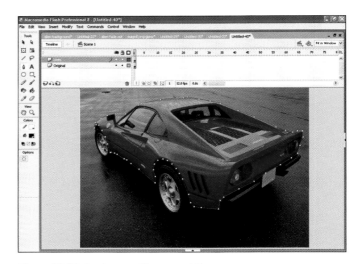

Figure 10.38 Create an outline around the car.

> If you prefer, you can create the outline using the Pencil tool or the Brush tool rather than using the Pen tool. Experiment with different thickness levels to see how it affects your final animation.

6. Create a new layer by clicking the Insert Layer button in the Layers palette.

7. Call the new layer "Mask."

8. Create a rectangle on the Mask layer similar to the one shown in Figure 10.39.

9. Right-click the Mask layer and choose Mask from the menu that appears.

10. Now it's time to animate your objects. To begin, right-click frame 10 in the Original layer and select Insert Keyframe from the menu that appears.

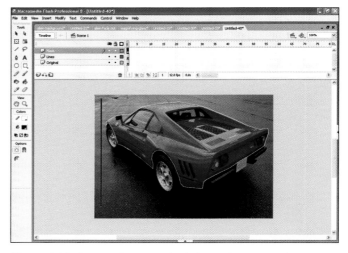

Figure 10.39 Create a thin rectangle similar to the one seen here.

11. Repeat step 10 on the Lines layer and the Mask layer. At this point, you should have three keyframes on frame 10, as shown in Figure 10.40.

12. Right-click any frame between frames 1 and 9 of the Mask layer and choose Create Motion Tween from the menu that appears to apply a motion tween to this layer.

13. To edit the motion tween, you'll need to unlock the layer. To begin, click frame 10 to select it.

14. Click the lock icon in the Mask layer to unlock the layer. You'll again see the rectangle the outline.

15. Using the Selection tool, move the rectangle to the opposite side of the Stage.

16. Click the lock icon to re-lock the layer.

17. Press Ctrl+Enter to play the animation. As the animation plays, the lines will appear animated around your object.

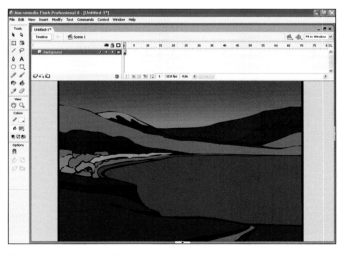

Figure 10.40 Create keyframes on frame 10 of each layer.

Tossing Rocks in a Pond

What could be more tranquil than throwing rocks into a pond and watching as the water ripples? You can re-create this tranquil scene in Flash through the creation of a few simple shape tweens. In this example I've created the ripple effect in a scene by animating some circles, but ultimately you can re-create this using any type of shape on any background.

1. Create a background for your image on a separate layer. For this example I've created the scene that is pictured in Figure 10.41, placing all the objects in the scene on a layer called "Background."

2. Create a new layer and call it "First Ripple."

Figure 10.41 Create a background image.

3. On the First Ripple layer, create a small oval, as shown in Figure 10.42.

4. Click frame 10 in the Background layer and press F6 to create a keyframe.

5. Repeat step 4 on frame 10 in the First Ripple layer.

6. Click frame 1 in the First Ripple layer and then open the Property inspector by pressing Ctrl+F3.

7. In the Tween drop-down list, choose Shape, as shown in Figure 10.43. Then click Ctrl+F3 to close the Property inspector.

8. Click frame 10 in the First Ripple layer.

9. Hold down the Alt key on your keyboard and use the Free Transform tool to expand the oval so that it takes up most of the pond, as shown in Figure 10.44.

10. Open the Color Mixer by pressing Shift+F9.

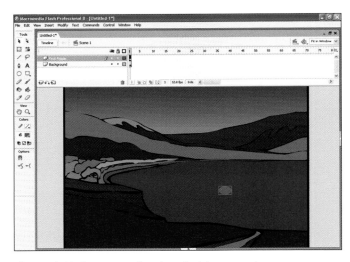

Figure 10.42 Create a small oval on the lake as seen here.

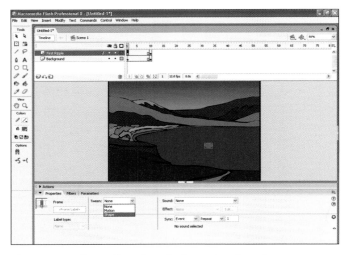

Figure 10.43 Choose Shape from the Tween drop-down list.

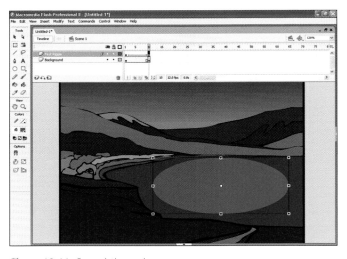

Figure 10.44 Expand the oval.

11. With the oval still selected, change the Alpha value to 0%, as shown in Figure 10.45. Then press Shift+F9 again to close the Color Mixer.

12. Press the Enter key to preview the animation. You should see the first ripple appear.

13. Your next task is to replicate this ripple, staggering it on several other layers. To begin, click and drag across frames 1–10 in the First Ripple layer to select them.

14. Press Ctrl+Alt+C to copy the selected frames.

15. Click frame 35 in the Background layer to select it.

16. Press F6 to extend the background to frame 35.

17. Create a new layer and name it "Second Ripple."

18. Click frame 5 in the Second Ripple layer and press Ctrl+Alt+V to paste the frames that you copied in step 14.

19. Because you pasted these frames on frame 5, the animation will appear staggered when played. To verify this, play the animation; you should see two ripples, one appearing slightly after the other, as in Figure 10.46.

20. Create two more layers, one called "Third Ripple" and the other called "Fourth Ripple."

21. Click frame 10 in the Third Ripple layer and press Ctrl+Alt+V to paste the copied frames.

22. Click frame 15 in the Fourth Ripple layer and press Ctrl+Alt+V to paste the copied frames (see Figure 10.47).

23. Play the animation; you should see a ripple with four ovals animated in a staggered manner.

Now You Try

Take the animation you just created one step further by adding to the beginning of the sequence a character throwing a rock into the pond at the point where the ripple starts. Try to create something similar to the character shown throwing a rock in Figure 10.48.

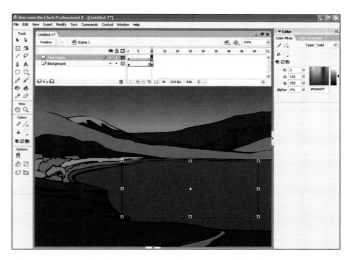

Figure 10.45 Make the oval completely see-through in frame 10 by changing its Alpha setting to 0%.

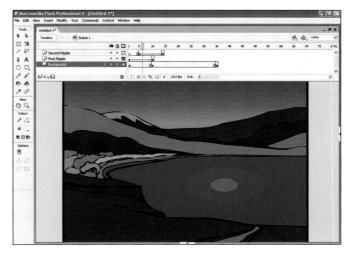

Figure 10.46 You should now see two ripples.

10. Cool Flash Effects

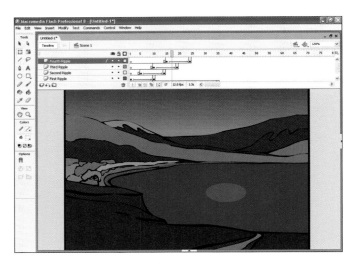

Figure 10.47 You should have four sets of ripples in the Timeline.

Figure 10.48 Add a character throwing a rock into the pond.

PRO • FILE

Name: Dermot O' Connor
Organization: idleworm
URL: http://www.idleworm.com/how/
index.shtml

How did you learn Flash? I used the book *Flash 4 for Windows and Macintosh*. It was part of the Visual Quickstart series of books. The manual was easy to follow, and well illustrated. I didn't take classes or learn from anyone...I just picked things up as I went along.

How did you get started using Flash? Once I had the book in my hands, it was easy. I was already a trained animator, so at first I used the program to assemble my hand-drawn animations. That took time, of course, as the drawings had to be "cleaned up"—drawn with a very solid black line, then scanned, and digitally colored. An old-school animator could use Flash just in that capacity and never bother with some of the program's more advanced features. Over a couple of years I realized that I could save a lot of time by cutting the character up onto layers. I began by removing a head and turning it into a symbol, repositioning it as the character moved. That way I could save myself hours of drawing, as well as reduce the file size. Then a light went off in my head, and I began to slice up the characters into many layers—one for the torso, one for the upper arm, one for the foot, one for the hand, etc. The process is analogous to rigging a character in 3D, and has been independently developed by many people, to differing extremes.

What feature/tool do you use most often? The ability to embed one animating symbol inside another is the single most powerful feature of the program. For example, I can create a mouth symbol, which says a line of dialogue. Then I can place the animated mouth in a head symbol, which can be rotated and motion-tweened as the character speaks. The head can be placed inside yet *another* symbol containing the entire body. This can go on indefinitely, allowing very rich animation to be created.

What do you like best about Flash? Speed and simplicity. Fifteen years ago we had to do everything by hand, including the inbe-tweens. Animation required as much stamina as skill. Today Flash "motion-tweens" for us; as recently as 10 years ago I had to create

these inbetweens by hand—a laborious process to put it mildly. I'm glad that I'll never have to do that again!

What sets your animations apart from others? Most people don't push Flash as far as I do in terms of shape tweening and "rigging" the characters (by which I mean separating them onto multiple layers). I have created a series of mouth shapes, which can blend into one another in any sequence—this allows for some very smooth dialogue scenes. My most intricate character had more than 100 layers. This layering is invisible to the viewer.

What is the secret to a great animation? Make the character appear to think. Disney old-timers called it "The Illusion of Life," and not everyone is capable of it. If you can make your characters feel alive, you're well on your way. It's the most difficult thing to do.

Are there any tips that you can share with the readers about using Flash?

1. Keep your files clean, by which I mean name your symbols carefully. You won't be able to progress far if your Library is full of objects called "Symbol 1," "Symbol 2," etc. Give your symbols meaningful names.

2. Avoid using the Group tool. Many use it as an alternative to creating symbols. The problem with this is that grouped objects can hide in a large file, making them difficult to manage. A symbol is much easier to detect, and global alterations to symbols are much easier.

3. Don't be afraid to experiment with shape tweening. It's a bit flaky, and often does things that are odd. The solution is to use shape hints, which can stabilize things. Be patient. If it doesn't work, try a different shape. Be warned: Flash can crash when you use shape hints, so be sure to back up your file first!

4. Sometimes you might want to do something a bit risky. In that case, you want to back-up your animation in case you want to revert to an earlier version. I create a layer, copy and paste the animation that I want to preserve onto it, and turn the layer into a "guide." Then I hide the layer. It won't export when I make an SWF, and I can restore the earlier version if I think I've messed things up.

Are there any animation tips you can share with our readers?
Always sketch out a quick thumbnail on paper. If you're having a problem with your work, there's no better way to diagnose the cause than to see a series of drawings on one page showing the action, comic-book style. You can make notes, add arrows showing the direction of movement, and even plan out some of the timing. This will make your final animation much richer and less mechanical.

Do you have any other advice for teens getting started with Flash animations? Don't be over ambitious. The biggest mistake you can make is to pick a project that is completely beyond your powers. Start with something that's just a little beyond what you think you can do. A good series of projects would look like this:

1. Animate a few scenes of basic actions: a bouncing ball, a person jumping in place, a walk cycle, a run cycle. Keep these designs simple—don't add lots of long hair or too much clothing. You'll have enough on your plate to begin with!

2. Animate a short, 10-second piece of a simple character, preferably doing something comical. This has to be a sequence that amuses you in some way—otherwise you'll lose interest very quickly.

3. Now you can scale up, tackling a 30-second piece. At this point you'll see if your organizational skills are adequate to the task. It's common to create a "scene list"—a table listing all the scenes in your movie, and what elements they'll need (backgrounds, effects, etc.). As you finish a scene, you tick it off on the list.

4. After 30 seconds, you'll have great respect for a one-minute animation—it doesn't sound like a lot, but it is. If you can animate a one-minute cartoon that holds people's attention, you're well on your way.

Many people stay at level 1. A large percentage of professional animators have never made their own movies; they simply work on the movies of others. It's up to you how far you want to move in the direction of animated films. The beauty of Flash is that it makes the creation of cartoons economical for all of us.

Samples

chapter 11
Help If You Need It

My goal writing this book is to give you a solid foundation for learning Flash—and with any luck, I've accomplished that. I'll be honest enough to tell you, however, that this book hasn't covered every feature of the program. So what's next? How do you bump from Flash amateur to Flash pro? The way I see it, the best way to progress from here is practice, practice, practice. The more animations you create, the more comfortable you'll feel with the program—and the more advanced the animations you'll be able to create. That being said, if you do get stuck at any point in the learning process, there are a variety of resources available to help you. Even if you *don't* get stuck, you may discover that you want to learn about features of the program that were not covered here, in which case these resources will prove useful. This chapter will show you where to get help with and how to learn more about Flash.

Using Flash's Internal Help

The fastest way to get help in Flash is to use the program's internal help feature, which you can launch at any time by pressing the F1 key. The Help window that appears is divided into two sections, as shown in Figure 11.1. The left side of the widow has different categories of subjects from which you can choose, and the right side of the window shows a full description of the subject you've selected.

Searching

At the top of the Help window you'll find the Search field, in which you can type the subject that you are looking for. For example, say you want to learn more about the ActionScript feature. To do so, type `Action Script` in the Search window and then click the Search button. A list of subjects that contain the word "Action" and/or the word "Script" appears. Now try the search again, but this time type `"Action Script"` with quotations around

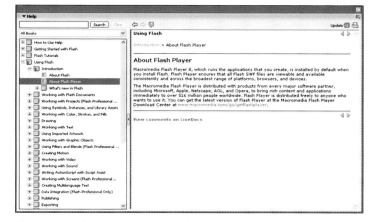

Figure 11.1 The Help window is split into two sections—topics on the left and descriptions on the right.

the words. When you receive the results of your search, you'll notice a lot fewer matches in the subject window (see Figure 11.2). That's because when you include quotations around your search terms, Flash will look for documents containing terms that exactly match the ones you type. (By the way, notice how even though you didn't use the official spelling of ActionScript, you still got the results you were looking for.)

When you find a subject that matches what you are looking for, click it; a description will appear in the right side of the window. At any point, you can click the Clear button (see Figure 11.3) to clear the search term and return to all the topics.

Browsing

Rather than looking for a specific topic, you may wish to simply browse through the categories of help subjects. To do so, simply click any of the main Help categories displayed in the left side of the Help window. (If the categories aren't displayed, try clicking the Clear button.) All the subjects under that category will appear, as shown in Figure 11.4.

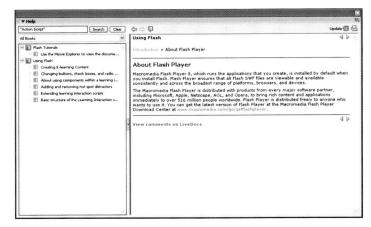

Figure 11.2 Adding quotations around your search terms prompts Flash's Help system to search for the exact phrase.

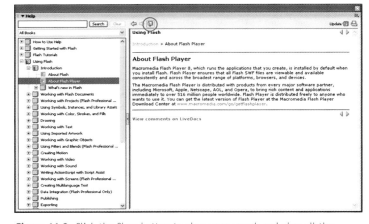

Figure 11.3 Click the Clear button to clear your search and view all the available Help topics.

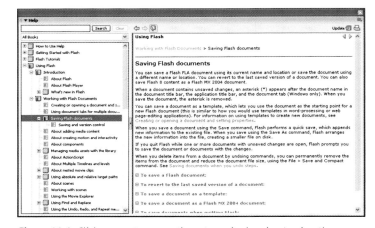

Figure 11.4 Click on a category or the category's plus sign to view the topics in that category.

If there is a little plus sign beside a category, it means that there are sub-categories within it. You can view these sub-categories by clicking the plus sign. When you find a subject you want to view, click it, and information about that subject will appear in the right side of the window. You can navigate the information in the right-hand pane by clicking the triangles in the top-right corner of the window, as shown in Figure 11.5.

Within some help topics, you might see little blue plus signs. These indicate that the topic can be expanded. You can reveal the expanded contents by clicking the plus sign.

Using Flash's Online Help

In addition to getting help within the program itself, Flash offers a web site from which you can access help files. To reach the site, click Flash's Help menu and choose Flash Support Center; this launches your default web browser with the Support Center page open (see Figure 11.6). Much like Flash's internal Help system, this web site allows you to enter specific help topics to search for. In addition to the help search functionality, this site offers a variety of other features including contacts, discussion groups, documentation, support, and user groups. I suggest you spend some time clicking the different links to see what's available.

Finding More Help Online

Before I get into finding additional online help, I want to issue a warning: When it comes to Flash and tutorials on the web, there is a lot of hype and very little substance. If you don't believe me, point your web browser to Google and type `Flash tutorials` or `Flash help`; hundreds if not thousands of links will appear. By the sheer number of links, you'd be reasonable to think that one of them would lead you to useful tutorials or information, but the unfortunate truth is that most free Flash help sites cover only the basics of Flash—which you've already learned in this book. If you're looking for help, my suggestion is stick to books and videos. If you insist on using the web, look for specific project tutorials. For example, say you see an interesting Flash effect—maybe a neat masking effect—on a web page that you want to replicate. Type a description of the effect in Google to see if you can find any tutorials that describe how to create it.

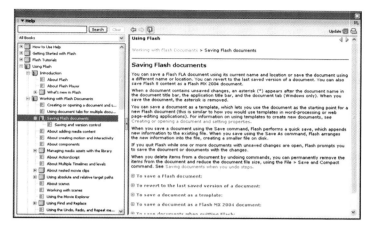

Figure 11.5 Use the arrow keys to navigate the help files.

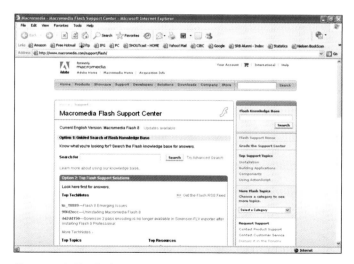

Figure 11.6 The Flash Support Center provides a variety of help resources.

That said, while the web might be short on helpful instructions, it's long on inspiration for your animations. Do a Google search on `cool Flash sites` or `Flash cartoons` and you'll find dozens of sites that you can use as inspiration.

Mining Flash Books and Videos

This book is meant to give you an introduction to Flash; other resources out there can take you in different directions or to more-advanced topics. Many of these resources also explore the myriad uses for Flash in more detail—for example, covering web animations only, focusing on Flash cartoons, outlining how you can use Flash to create games, and so on. To help you move to the next level of Flash animation, I've provided a list of other resources available from Thompson Course:

◆ *Macromedia Flash 8 Revealed, Deluxe Education Edition* by James Shuman. ISBN: 1-4188-4309-1.

◆ *Macromedia Flash 8 Interactive Movie Tutorials, Starter* by James Shuman. ISBN: 1-4188-6011-5.

◆ *Macromedia Studio 8 Step-by-Step: Projects for Dreamweaver 8, Fireworks 8, Flash 8, and Contribute 3* by Jay Heins, Scott Tapley, and Skipper Pickle. ISBN: 0-619-26709-7

◆ *CourseCard: Flash MX 2004*. ISBN: 0-619-28687-3.

◆ *Course ILT: Flash MX: Basic with CD + CBT*. ISBN: 1-4188-4522-1.

◆ *Course ILT: Flash MX 2004 Advanced*. ISBN: 0-619-20419-2.

Obviously, there are dozens of other resources available from other publishers both online and in bookstores. Once you determine the specific area in which you would like more help, I encourage you to explore these different resources.

Index

G

ghost typing effects, 155–159
Goldwave software, 33
gradient fills
  applying, 83
  colors, changing, 84
  modifying, 84–85
  preset, 83–84
  types, changing, 84
Gradient Transform tool, 84–85
grouping objects, 81
growing objects, 8
guide layers, 98

H

Hand tool, 30
header, Timeline, 18
height of animation settings, 25
Heins, Jay, 182
help options
  books, 182
  browsing, 180–181
  contacts, 181
  discussion groups, 181
  documentation, 181
  Flash Support Center, 181
  online help, 181
  resources, 182
  searches, 179–180
  support, 181
  tutorials, 181
  user groups, 181
  videos, 182

Hide Layer button, 94
hiding
  layers, 94
  Property inspector, 22
  Timeline, 20
Hit button-state option, 150
horizontal alignment, 60

I

idleworm web site, 177
ImageReady software, 33
images, importing, 56–57
Import dialog box, 56–57, 162
importing
  objects, 56–57
  sounds, 141–142
indicators, Timeline, 18
Ink Bottle tool, 74–75, 77
Insert Layer button, 98, 143
inspectors, opening, closing, and repositioning, 23

J

JibJab web site, 89

K

keyboard
  keyboard shortcut keys, menus, 15
  selecting frames using, 31
keyframes
  blank, 99
  creating multiple, 101–102
  defined, 17, 99

L

Lasso tool
  moving objects with, 59
  selecting objects with, 54
launching Flash, 11
Layer Folder button, 96
Layer Properties dialog box, 98
layers
  cells *versus*, 91
  creating, 91–93
  deleting, 96
  discussed, 16
  folder organization, 96–97
  guide, 98
  hiding, 94
  locking/unlocking, 94–95
  mask effects and, 164–165
  moving, 93
  moving objects to different layers, 95
  naming, 91–93
  New Layer button, 91–92
  order of, changing, 93
  properties, changing, 98
  removing from folders, 97
Layers area, Timeline features, 16
layouts, saving, 24
Left Channel sound-effect option, 148
Library dialog box, 142
lightsabers, sound effects, 148
Line tool, 45
lines, drawing
  color, size, and style changes, 45
  line properties, changing, 43
  smooth lines, 42
  straight lines, 40–41
  using Pen tool, 46–47

Index

Flash Animation for Teens

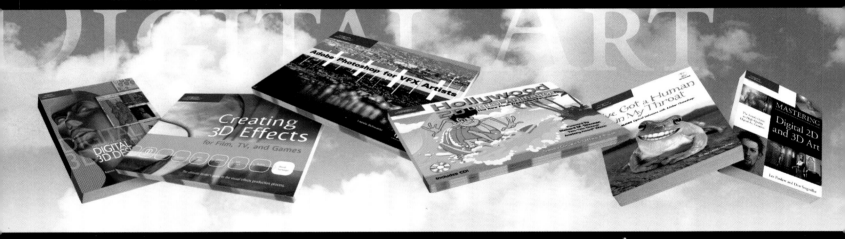